· THE ONLY ·

# Bake Sale Cookbook

· YOU'LL EVER NEED ·

# 201 Mouthwatering, Kid-Pleasing Treats

*wm*

WILLIAM MORROW
*An Imprint of* HarperCollins*Publishers*

### · THE ONLY ·

## Bake Sale Cookbook

### · YOU'LL EVER NEED ·

## LAURIE GOLDRICH WOLF *and* PAM ABRAMS

HarperCollins books may be purchased for educational, business, or sales promotional use. For information please write: Special Markets Department, HarperCollins Publishers, 10 East 53rd Street, New York, NY 10022.

FIRST EDITION

*Designed by Jessica Shatan Heslin/Studio Shatan, Inc.*

*Produced by Downtown Bookworks Inc.*

Library of Congress Cataloging-in-Publication Data has been applied for.

ISBN 978-0-06-123383-8

08  09  10  11  12  WBC/QW  10  9  8  7  6  5  4  3  2  1

*To my wonderful father, Nathaniel Goldrich, who was always honest, always funny, and always had room for another piece of cake. I love you, Dad. And to Ella, for letting my family and me see that angels do exist.*
—L.G.W.

*To my parents, Ken and Madeline, who taught me the value of activism and the joy of the kitchen.*
—P.A.

# • CONTENTS •

# ACKNOWLEDGMENTS

We have worked on many projects together over the last thirteen years and have always been great collaborators, so first and foremost we acknowledge each other. There is nothing quite as gratifying as working with a friend whose talents complement your own. Writing a book about things that taste good is destined to bring out the best in people—which is just what happened. We had the good fortune to work with Harriet Bell and Sarah Durand at William Morrow—their enthusiasm for the project kept us happily up to our elbows in flour. Julie Merberg and Patty Brown at Downtown Bookworks provided unwavering support as we worked on this book, as did Sara Newberry, upon whose culinary eagle eye we heavily relied. Thanks, too, to the folks at Share Our Strength and MoveOn.org, whose bake sale savvy inspired us.

Laurie would also like to acknowledge the following people: Freddi, David, and the kids; Janet, John, and the boys; all the Ponces; my pseudo kids, Katie and Matt; Fred and Geri; my husband, Bruce; and my wonderful children, Olivia and Nick. You are all awesome.

· THE ONLY ·

Bake Sale Cookbook

· YOU'LL EVER NEED ·

# · INTRODUCTION ·

*When it comes to volunteering, some of us to like to* make signs or run fairs—and some of us like to put on an apron and preheat the oven. If, like us, you fall into the latter category, this book's for you. As bakers and parents, we feel really good when we contribute home-baked goods to help raise money for a cause.

Over the years we have baked to support fund-raisers at our kids' schools, for political campaigns, to support community events, or to raise money to donate to groups we like. We've participated in The Great American Bake Sale organized by the nonprofit group Share Our Strength (for more information visit www.greatamericanbakesale .org), and MoveOn.org's Bake Sale for Democracy, and a post-9/11 sale to benefit our local firehouse. And sometimes we just bake with our kids and let them set up shop with cookies and lemonade on the front steps. Collected here are the 201 recipes for treats that pass the Bake Sale Test: They're portable, delicious, and look great.

## WHY BAKE SALES WORK

Everyone—buyer and baker alike—loves a bake sale. It's an event that brings people together in the spirit of volunteerism. The best bake sales rely on a team of people who can split up the tasks. Don't try to do it all yourself!

Traditionally, schools have been the venue for bake sales, and these days, with school budgets being slashed, PTOs and PTAs are filling the gap more than ever. Kids, teachers, staff, and parents make an ever-present captive audience, so schools are ideal locations.

But bake sales are popping up in all kinds of places now: farmers' markets, busy intersections, soccer games, front lawns—virtually anyplace where communities congregate. There are no rules: Raise money for yourself or a cause you believe in; involve your kids or your best friends; hold a bake sale any time of year, indoors or out. There's little to no overhead, so profits can go right to your bottom line.

Below are strategies for successful sales, from veterans and newcomers alike.

## SOLICITING DONATIONS

Successful sales, of course, depend on successful donations. And there is an art to asking people to bake for you. Our ten best tips:

- **Reach out via multiple streams**. E-mail, notices in kids' backpacks, phone, posters, blogs.

- **Emphasize where the proceeds will go**. Bakers are more likely to participate if they're supporting something they care about.

- **Give bakers some suggestions**. You might want to give people a few ideas on what to bake. If it's a daytime sale suggest muffins or banana bread. For preschoolers, it's all about the sprinkles.

- **Solicit 25 percent more product than you need.** Inevitably some people will commit to participating but not be able to come through.

- **Think outside the box** when it comes to whom to solicit. If you know a talented baker, he or she will probably be flattered by a personal phone call requesting a delicious donation.

- **Give two to three weeks' notice.** Then remind them again a week before and the day before. E-mail is your friend here.

- **Encourage homemade.** Tell people that you'll be able to charge more for home-baked than store-bought goods—even if they're not totally from scratch.

- **Engage your elders.** Know a grandmother who likes to bake? Tap the seniors in your area to contribute to a sale—like a school fund-raiser—even if they're not in the sale's audience. People who like to bake often just need to be asked and will gladly participate.

- **Be prepared to accept alternative contributions.** Give people the option to help out in other ways if they can't bake for the sale. Every sale needs napkins, plates, and paper cups. Or maybe you need help to set up, publicize, clean up, etc.

- **Tap kids!** Sometimes it's better to ask the kids rather than the adults in the household to bake for a sale. Teenagers are often competent bakers and will contribute if asked (especially if it's by someone other than their own parent).

- **Thank everyone afterward.** They will be grateful to know how it went and more inclined to participate next time.

## FUND-RAISING POTENTIAL

So, how much money can you really net at a bake sale? It depends on how many baked goods you have, how many potential customers you reach, how long your sale lasts. But here are ways to maximize your profits:

- **Have good food.** In the end, it's always about quality.

- **Choose a high-traffic location** such as a busy hallway, a corner with people coming from two directions, outside a popular store, in the parking lot outside a well-attended game, at the intermission of a community or school performance, or a table at a fair or carnival. Every August, during the horse-racing season in Saratoga Springs, New York, kids set up bake sales on the sidewalk leading out of the track. At about 5 P.M., as hundreds of hot and hungry patrons leave the racetrack, lemonade and brownies sell briskly.

- **Be passionate about your cause.** The more impassioned you (and your community) are, the more successful your sale will be. Always make it very clear what you're raising money for: Make signs and display them clearly. And consider the buyers in your audience. If the cause is one they support, they will be more likely to say "keep the change."

- **Have the right food for the right audience.** Brightly colored (especially blue!) treats are like magnets for preschool and elementary-school buyers. Coffee cakes do very well at morning or daytime events.

- **Invest a little.** At most sales the overhead is low: paper plates, plastic forks, napkins, tablecloths. Sometimes you can ask for these as donations and keep all your profits. But don't be afraid to invest a little more to make your sale appealing (it is food, after all). A pretty tablecloth and a coffee can full of fresh flowers can make all the difference in attracting people to your table.

- **Serve drinks.** You can buy a case of single-serve water bottles and mark them up slightly to sell individually. A bowl or pitchers of homemade punch are inexpensive to make, and can really boost the profits at your sale.

## SETTING UP YOUR TABLE

As we've mentioned, pretty tables and nice signs draw buyers to your table. Here are a few setups that will help your sale:

- **Tap artistic friends to do the signage.** Or employ kids and ask them to use lots of color.

- **Make your cause known** on the signs. Whether the money is going to the PTA or the Environmental Defense Fund, be bold and clear in the lettering.

- **Hang a banner** over your table, if possible. It's a great way to attract attention.

- **Use a tablecloth.** Baked goods are usually more appealing when served on a cloth. We like the colorful, wipe-clean kind made of oilcloth or plastic. If you're serving drinks, definitely don't use paper. And if the sale is going to go on for hours you may want to bring along two tablecloths and use a fresh one halfway through.

- **Be creative when naming your goods.** At a MoveOn bake sale the Condoleezza Rice Krispie Treats were bestsellers!

- **Start with change**. Make sure you have plenty of $1 bills—you don't want to have to turn early buyers away because you can't make change. We recommend starting with at least $20 in singles and $5 worth of quarters, nickels, and dimes.

- **State your prices in writing**—it will save your server(s) a lot of hassle.

- **If you have beverages** that are hard to see (in a cooler under the table, perhaps) make sure to have a sign or small display that lets people know they're available.

- **Bring serving dishes**—we like oversize plastic platters, available at party stores. It's also nice to have a few assorted cake plates from home, which are much nicer-looking than paper plates. Whatever you do, don't serve out of Tupperware!

- **Set up multiple levels**. Tiered plates are ideal for bake sales because they create visual interest. Tiered cupcake holders, cake stands, and portable shelves can help you set up a really nice-looking table. (See Resources, page 247.)

- **Have a few knives and spatulas handy,** and bring a couple of rolls of paper towels along, too. (You can never have too many paper towels.)

- **Keep your table neat and clean** as the day goes on. Wipe off crumbs, keep plates filled, clean up spills, etc. You want to make everyone who walks over feel like they're in a really appealing bakery.

- **Have plastic bins or boxes** to keep donations in.

- **Don't put everything out at once**, but keep your table well stocked throughout the day.

- **Work in shifts.** If your sale lasts more than an hour or two you'll want to stagger shifts. It's easier to get volunteers to commit to short blocks of time.

## PUBLICIZING YOUR BAKE SALE

Use all available media to let people know about your sale: word of mouth, signs, flyers, e-mail blasts, newsletters, ads, e-vites, etc. Don't be shy about calling the press to cover your event; often they love a local do-gooder story. Just figure out the hook (famous bakers, good cause, kid involvement) and pitch your story.

## FIGURING OUT HOW MUCH YOU NEED

There's no simple answer to this question, but think about these things to help you figure out the answer.

- **Ask around.** Do you know anyone who has done a bake sale in the same location? If so, ask them how much they sold. Better yet, do a sale, learn from your experience, and then do it again.

- **Rule of thumb:** one large or two small baked goods per potential customer who may walk by. Estimating the potential crowd is the trick.

- **Be prepared to donate leftovers** to a shelter or food pantry in your area. Call up beforehand to see if they'll accept donations, then make it someone's job to deliver the goods.

## TRANSPORT TIPS

There are some indispensable products when it comes to transporting baked goods to a sale. Our top picks:

- **Cupcake carriers and cake savers** (see Resources, page 247) are wonderful because goods stay fresh and frosting undisturbed. They're worth the investment if you bake and carry more than once a year.

- **Shirt boxes and shoeboxes,** when lined with aluminum foil, make excellent carriers for cookies, bars, and brownies. Put a sheet of parchment paper or wax paper in between the layers.

- **Buy inexpensive plastic containers in bulk.** Disposable plastic containers (the kind you buy in the supermarket) make it easy to drop off a donation.

- **A rimmed cookie sheet** is a good way to send a tray full of muffins or cupcakes to a bake sale. If they're iced, insert toothpicks into the corner cupcakes, and cover loosely with foil or plastic wrap.

And finally: Have fun! The core of a bake sale is that it inspires a sense of camaraderie and community. Don't underestimate that benefit when you agree to participate. Take pictures, inspire your friends, include your kids. Bake sales are good for you.

# One

## 23 Varieties of Rice Krispie Treats

*Why is this old-fashioned dessert the number one bestseller at bake sales? Probably because you either loved these treats when you were a kid, or you are a kid. We love them because they're incredibly easy to make. The basic recipe lends itself to much creative interpretation, as you'll see from the twenty-three varieties here. And once you've tried them, make up your own.*

# · RICE KRISPIE CHOCOLATE ROLL ·

*This jelly roll–like variation on the Rice Krispie square is made with a rich chocolate filling. Slice the roll at your bake sale or ahead of time. The spirals inside the roll look cool—and taste delicious!*

## Makes 15 slices

1 cup white corn syrup
1 cup smooth peanut butter
1 cup granulated sugar
3 tablespoons unsalted butter
6 cups rice cereal

*Filling*
2 cups confectioners' sugar
1 cup unsweetened cocoa powder
$\frac{1}{2}$ cup (1 stick) unsalted butter, softened
$\frac{1}{4}$ cup water
2 teaspoons vanilla extract

**1.** Line a baking sheet with wax paper. Stir together the corn syrup, peanut butter, sugar, and butter in a heavy saucepan. Heat over medium heat. Bring to a boil and remove from the heat.

**2.** Add the cereal and stir until it is well coated. Pour the mixture out onto the lined pan. With your hands, press the mixture into a 10×15-inch rectangle. (It helps if you do this with damp hands.) Allow it to sit for 20 minutes. It should still be warm and pliable.

**3.** Make the filling: In a large bowl, combine the confectioners' sugar, cocoa, butter, water, and vanilla. Beat with an electric mixer on high speed until smooth, 5 to 7 minutes. The filling should be the consistency of frosting. If the filling is too stiff to spread, stir in water a teaspoon at a time until it reaches spreading consistency.

**4.** With a spatula, spread the filling over the cereal mixture in an even layer. Roll up like a jelly roll from the long end. Wrap tightly in plastic wrap and chill for at least 1 hour.

**5.** Slice into 1-inch slices with a serrated knife, dipping the blade in warm water and wiping it dry between cuts.

# · PB AND BUTTERSCOTCH ·

*Who needs jelly when you can have butterscotch instead? These decadent treats work equally well with chunky or smooth peanut butter.*

## Makes 12 bars

| | |
|---|---|
| 2 cups (12 ounces) butterscotch chips | 2 cups (12 ounces) semisweet chocolate chips |
| 1 cup peanut butter | 1 cup confectioners' sugar |
| 8 cups rice cereal | $^1/_4$ cup ($^1/_2$ stick) unsalted butter |

**1.** Coat a 9×13-inch baking pan with cooking spray and set aside.

**2.** Combine the butterscotch chips and the peanut butter in a large nonstick saucepan and heat over low heat, stirring until smooth.

**3.** Remove the pan from the heat and add the rice cereal and stir until well mixed. Press half of the mixture evenly into the pan. Chill until set, about 20 minutes.

**4.** Heat the chocolate chips, sugar, butter, and 2 tablespoons water in a small saucepan over low heat, stirring until melted.

**5.** Spread the chocolate mixture on the cereal mixture in the pan. Press the remaining cereal evenly over the top. Chill until set, about 20 minutes, before cutting into 3×3$^1/_4$-inch bars.

**TIP**
Rice Krispie Treats look very appealing if you wrap slices or squares individually in colored cellophane and tie each end with ribbon. Look for cellophane in pretty pale colors that you can see through.

# · CONFETTI BARS ·

*Depending on the colors of the sprinkles you choose, these can be tailored for a specific holiday. Multicolored sprinkles are a sure hit year-round.*

*Makes 12 bars*

| | |
|---|---|
| $\frac{1}{4}$ cup ($\frac{1}{2}$ stick) unsalted butter | 7 cups rice cereal |
| One 10-ounce package marshmallows | $\frac{1}{2}$ cup multicolored candy sprinkles |

**1.** Spray a $9 \times 13$-inch baking pan with cooking spray and set aside.

**2.** Heat the butter in a large nonstick saucepan over low heat until melted. Add the marshmallows and continue cooking, stirring until smooth, 2 to 3 minutes.

**3.** Remove the pan from the heat and stir in the cereal, then the sprinkles, stirring to mix well.

**4.** Press the mixture evenly into the prepared pan. Cool completely, about 20 minutes, before cutting into $3 \times 3\frac{1}{4}$-inch bars.

# · TRIPLE THREATS ·

*Nuts, raisins, and dried cranberries pack a tasty punch in these crispy treats.*
*You can substitute chocolate-covered raisins for plain ones if you prefer.*

## Makes 12 bars

| | |
|---|---|
| ¼ cup (½ stick) unsalted butter | 1 cup salted peanuts |
| One 10-ounce package | 1 cup raisins |
| marshmallows | 1 cup dried cranberries |
| 4 cups rice cereal | |

**1.** Spray a 9×13-inch baking pan with cooking spray and set aside.

**2.** Heat the butter in a large nonstick saucepan over low heat until melted. Add the marshmallows and continue cooking, stirring until smooth, 2 to 3 minutes.

**3.** Remove the pan from the heat and stir in the cereal, peanuts, raisins, and cranberries until well mixed.

**4.** Press the mixture evenly into the prepared pan. Cool completely before cutting into 3×3¼-inch bars, about 20 minutes.

# · LOVE ME DO ·

*Heavenly treats for a Valentine's Day bake sale, but take it from us:*
*These edible love notes sell anytime, anywhere.*

## Makes about twenty-five 2-inch hearts

| | |
|---|---|
| 3 tablespoons unsalted butter | Prepared cake frosting |
| One 10-ounce package | Red decorating gel |
|    marshmallows | Assorted red candies (Red Hots, |
| 6 cups rice cereal |    gum drops, jelly beans, etc.) |

**1.** Spray a 15 × 10-inch baking pan with cooking spray and set aside.

**2.** Heat the butter in a large nonstick saucepan over low heat until melted. Add the marshmallows and continue cooking, stirring until smooth, 2 to 3 minutes.

**3.** Remove the pan from the heat and stir in the cereal until well mixed.

**4.** Press the mixture evenly into the prepared pan. Cool completely before cutting into hearts, about 20 minutes.

**5.** Using a 2-inch heart-shaped cookie cutter, cut as many hearts as you can from the pan. Decorate using the frosting, gel, and assorted candies.

> **TIP**
>
> If you use more than one color of frosting, use a different pastry bag for each color. You can also fit the pastry bag with a star or leaf tip. Remember: The decorating gel will not harden, but the frosting will.

# · PRESENT TIME ·

*These treats wrap up beautifully and always look appealing at a bake sale. We have decorated them as holiday gifts for a winter sale, and pretty packages at other times of year.*

## Makes about twenty-four 2-inch gifts

| | |
|---|---|
| 3 tablespoons unsalted butter | Assorted holiday candies (jelly |
| One 10-ounce package | beans, candy canes, chocolate |
| marshmallows | bells) |
| 6 cups rice cereal | Red string licorice |

**1.** Spray a 9×13-inch baking pan with cooking spray and set aside.

**2.** Heat the butter in a large nonstick saucepan over low heat until melted. Add the marshmallows and continue cooking, stirring until smooth, 2 to 3 minutes.

**3.** Remove the pan from the heat and add the rice cereal. Stir until well mixed.

**4.** Press the mixture evenly into the prepared pan. Cool completely before cutting into shapes, about 20 minutes.

**5.** Cut the treats into shapes, preferably squares and rectangles, to resemble gift boxes. Decorate with candies and tie with the string licorice to look like ribbon. (If the candy doesn't stick to the gifts, secure with a dab of water.)

# · RICE KRISPIE DOUGHNUTS ·

*Sell these as singles or by the dozen. And you can sell the "holes"
for a quarter apiece.*

*Makes thirty-two 2-inch doughnuts*

¼ cup (½ stick) unsalted butter, plus
    more for your hands
One 10-ounce package
    marshmallows

1 teaspoon vanilla extract
6 cups rice cereal
Chocolate sprinkles, colored
    sprinkles, and confectioners' sugar

**1.** Spray a 9×13-inch baking sheet with cooking spray and set aside.

**2.** Heat the butter in a large nonstick saucepan over low heat until melted. Add the marshmallows and continue cooking, stirring until smooth, 2 to 3 minutes.

**3.** Remove the pan from the heat and stir in the vanilla. Add the rice cereal and stir until well mixed.

**4.** Butter your hands and break the rice mixture into Ping-Pong-size balls. Flatten the balls into disks and make a hole in the middle to form doughnut shapes.

**5.** Top the doughnuts by pressing the sprinkles or sugar around the entire doughnut. Allow to set completely, about 20 minutes.

# · RICE KRISPIE DOUBLE DECKERS ·

*Makes 12 bars*

½ cup (1 stick) unsalted butter, divided in half

Two 10-ounce packages marshmallows

6 cups rice cereal

One 1-pound container milk chocolate frosting

6 cups chocolate rice cereal

**1.** Spray a 9×13-inch baking pan with cooking spray and set aside.

**2.** Heat one half of the butter in a large nonstick saucepan over low heat until melted. Add 1 package of marshmallows and continue cooking, stirring until smooth, 2 to 3 minutes.

**3.** Remove the pan from the heat and add the rice cereal. Stir until well mixed.

**4.** Press the mixture evenly into the prepared pan. Cool completely until set, about 20 minutes.

**5.** Spread the chocolate frosting over the first layer and place in the refrigerator for 30 minutes.

**6.** Repeat steps 2 and 3 with the remaining butter and marshmallows, and the chocolate rice cereal.

**7.** Press the chocolate cereal in an even layer over the chocolate frosting. Chill in the refrigerator until set, at least 30 minutes, before cutting into 3×3¼-inch bars.

# · RK M&M TREATS ·

| | |
|---|---|
| ¼ cup (½ stick) unsalted butter | ½ cup peanut butter |
| One 10-ounce package marshmallows | 5 cups rice cereal |
| | 1½ cups M&M's |

**1.** Spray a 9×13-inch baking pan with cooking spray and set aside.

**2.** Heat the butter in a large nonstick saucepan over low heat until melted. Stir in the peanut butter. Add the marshmallows and continue cooking, stirring until smooth, 2 to 3 minutes.

**3.** Remove the pan from the heat and add the rice cereal and the M&M's. Stir until well mixed.

**4.** Press the mixture evenly into the prepared pan. Cool completely until set, about 20 minutes, before cutting into 3×3¼-inch bars.

# · CHEERY-OS ·

*Even the biggest fans of Rice Krispie Treats sometimes appreciate a change.*

## Makes 12 bars

| | |
|---|---|
| ¼ cup (½ stick) unsalted butter | ½ cup Nutella |
| One 10-ounce package marshmallows | 8 cups Cheerios or other O-shaped cereal |

**1.** Spray a 9×13-inch baking pan with cooking spray and set aside.

**2.** Heat the butter in a large nonstick saucepan over low heat until melted. Add the marshmallows and the Nutella; continue cooking, stirring until smooth, 2 to 3 minutes.

**3.** Remove the pan from the heat, add the Cheerios, and stir until well mixed.

**4.** Press the mixture evenly into the prepared pan. Cool completely until set, about 20 minutes, before cutting into 3×3¼-inch bars.

# · FRUITY GRANOLA TREATS ·

*Makes 12 bars*

| | |
|---|---|
| ¼ cup (½ stick) unsalted butter | 6 cups granola |
| One 10-ounce package | ½ cup chopped dates |
|    marshmallows | ½ cup chopped dried apricots |

**1.** Spray a 9×13-inch baking pan with cooking spray and set aside.

**2.** Heat the butter in a large nonstick saucepan over low heat until melted. Add the marshmallows and continue cooking, stirring until smooth, 2 to 3 minutes.

**3.** Remove the pan from the heat, add the granola and the dried fruit, and stir until well mixed.

**4.** Press the mixture evenly into the prepared pan. Cool completely until set, about 20 minutes, before cutting into 3×3¼-inch bars.

# · COCONUT KRISPIES ·

*Makes 12 bars*

| | |
|---|---|
| ¼ cup (½ stick) unsalted butter | 1 cup sweetened flaked coconut |
| One 10-ounce package | 1 cup (6 ounces) chocolate chips |
| marshmallows | ½ cup chopped toasted almonds |
| 6 cups rice cereal | |

**1.** Spray a 9×13-inch baking pan with cooking spray and set aside.

**2.** Heat the butter in a large nonstick saucepan over low heat until melted. Add the marshmallows and continue cooking, stirring until smooth, 2 to 3 minutes.

**3.** Remove from the heat, add the cereal, coconut, chocolate chips, and almonds, and stir until well mixed.

**4.** Press the mixture evenly into the prepared pan. Cool completely until set, about 20 minutes, before cutting into 3×3¼-inch bars.

**TIP**

These are especially delicious when made with toasted coconut: Spread sweetened flaked coconut on an ungreased baking sheet and toast at 350°F until golden, about 5 minutes.

# · CARAMEL KRISPIES ·

*Makes 12 bars*

| | |
|---|---|
| 2 tablespoons (¼ stick) unsalted butter | ½ cup prepared caramel sauce |
| One 10-ounce package marshmallows | 3½ cups rice cereal |
| | 3½ cups chocolate rice cereal |

**1.** Spray a 9×13-inch baking pan with cooking spray and set aside.

**2.** Heat the butter in a large nonstick saucepan over low heat until melted. Add the marshmallows and continue cooking, stirring until smooth, 2 to 3 minutes. Stir in the caramel sauce.

**3.** Remove the pan from the heat, add the cereals, and stir until well mixed.

**4.** Press the mixture evenly into the prepared pan. Cool completely until set, about 20 minutes, before cutting into 3×3¼-inch bars.

# · OREO TREATS ·

*We like to keep the Oreos in big chunks; it's kind of like finding
the big chunks of cookie dough in that great ice cream!*

## Makes 12 bars

| | |
|---|---|
| ¼ cup (½ stick) unsalted butter | 5 cups rice cereal |
| One 10-ounce package marshmallows | 2½ cups Oreo cookies, cut into quarters |

**1.** Spray a 9×13-inch baking pan with cooking spray and set aside.

**2.** Heat the butter in a large nonstick saucepan over low heat until melted. Add the marshmallows and continue cooking, stirring until smooth, 2 to 3 minutes.

**3.** Remove the pan from the heat, add the cereal and cookies, and stir gently just until mixed, to avoid breaking up the cookies any further.

**4.** Press the mixture evenly into the prepared pan. Cool completely until set, about 20 minutes, before cutting into 3×3¼-inch bars.

# · RED, WHITE, AND BLUE BARS ·

*These sell well at Election Day bake sales or around the Fourth of July at outdoor fairs. What could be more patriotic?*

*Makes 12 bars*

| | |
|---|---|
| ¼ cup (½ stick) unsalted butter | ½ cup dried blueberries |
| One 10-ounce package marshmallows | ½ cup chopped dried strawberries |
| 6 cups rice cereal | ½ cup white chocolate chips |
| | Red, white, and blue candy sprinkles |

**1.** Spray a 9×13-inch baking pan with cooking spray and set aside.

**2.** Heat the butter in a large nonstick saucepan over low heat until melted. Add the marshmallows and continue cooking, stirring until smooth, 2 to 3 minutes.

**3.** Remove the pan from the heat, add the cereal, dried fruit, and white chocolate chips, and stir until well mixed.

**4.** Press the mixture evenly into the prepared pan. Decorate with sprinkles, pressing down gently to make them stick. Cool completely until set, about 20 minutes, before cutting into 3×3¼-inch bars.

# · COCOA MINT KRISPIES ·

*A slight variation on the theme, and a delicious one.*

## Makes 12 bars

¼ cup (½ stick) unsalted butter
One 10-ounce package
   marshmallows
1 teaspoon peppermint extract
7 cups chocolate rice cereal

1 cup chopped chocolate-covered
   soft mints
1 tube chocolate frosting
24 Junior Mints

**1.** Spray a 9×13-inch baking pan with cooking spray and set aside.

**2.** Heat the butter in a large nonstick saucepan over low heat until melted. Add the marshmallows and continue cooking, stirring until smooth, 2 to 3 minutes, then stir in the peppermint extract.

**3.** Remove the pan from the heat, add the cereal and the chopped mints, and stir until well mixed.

**4.** Press the mixture evenly into the prepared pan. Cool completely until set, about 20 minutes, before cutting into squares.

**5.** Cut into 3×3¼-inch bars, then squirt a small blob of frosting on the top of each, and top with a Junior Mint.

# • S'MORE TREATS •

*Makes 12 bars*

| | |
|---|---|
| ¼ cup (½ stick) unsalted butter | 4 cups rice cereal |
| One 10-ounce package marshmallows | 2 cups Golden Grahams cereal |
| | 1 cup (6 ounces) chocolate chips |

**1.** Spray a 9×13-inch baking pan with cooking spray and set aside.

**2.** Heat the butter in a large nonstick saucepan over low heat until melted. Add the marshmallows and continue cooking, stirring until smooth, 2 to 3 minutes.

**3.** Remove the pan from the heat, add both cereals and the chocolate chips, and stir until well mixed.

**4.** Press the mixture evenly into the prepared pan. Cool completely until set, about 20 minutes, before cutting into 3×3¼-inch bars.

# · TURTLE TREATS ·

*Makes 12 bars*

| | |
|---|---|
| ¼ cup (½ stick) unsalted butter | 6 cups rice cereal |
| One 10-ounce package marshmallows | 1 cup chopped toasted pecans |
| | 1 cup (6 ounces) milk chocolate chips, melted |

**1.** Spray a 9×13-inch baking pan with cooking spray and set aside.

**2.** Heat the butter in a large nonstick saucepan over low heat until melted. Add the marshmallows and continue cooking, stirring until smooth, 2 to 3 minutes.

**3.** Remove the pan from the heat, add the cereal and the pecans, and stir until well mixed.

**4.** Press the mixture evenly into the prepared pan. Cool completely until set, about 20 minutes. Drizzle with the melted chocolate chips and let the chocolate set completely, about 20 minutes, before cutting into 3×3¼-inch bars.

**TIP**

To toast pecans, spread them evenly in a single layer on a cookie sheet and bake at 325°F for 7 to 10 minutes. Stir occasionally.

# · FROOT LOOP FUN ·

*The color of these squares sends grown-ups straight back to childhood and children straight to heaven.*

---

## Makes 12 bars

¼ cup (½ stick) unsalted butter
One 10-ounce package
   marshmallows

7 cups Froot Loops cereal

**1.** Spray a 9×13-inch baking pan with cooking spray and set aside.

**2.** Heat the butter in a large nonstick saucepan over low heat until melted. Add the marshmallows and continue cooking, stirring until smooth, 2 to 3 minutes.

**3.** Remove the pan from the heat, add the cereal, and stir until well mixed.

**4.** Press the mixture evenly into the prepared pan. Cool completely until set, about 20 minutes, then cut into 3×3¼-inch bars.

# · RICE KRISPIE POPS ·

*Consider this an edible crafts project as well as a bake sale winner.*
*Craft sticks are available at most arts-and-crafts supply stores.*

## Makes 12 pops

| | |
|---|---|
| ¼ cup (½ stick) unsalted butter | 7 cups rice cereal |
| One 10-ounce package marshmallows | 12 lollipop or craft sticks |
| | 2 cups (12 ounces) chocolate candy melts |

**1.** Spray a 9×13-inch baking pan with cooking spray and set aside.

**2.** Heat the butter in a large nonstick saucepan over low heat until melted. Add the marshmallows and continue cooking, stirring until smooth, 2 to 3 minutes.

**3.** Remove the pan from the heat, add the cereal, and stir until well mixed.

**4.** Press the mixture evenly into the prepared pan. Cool completely until set, about 20 minutes. Cut the mixture in half lengthwise, then into rectangles measuring about 2 inches by 4 inches.

**5.** Press a lollipop or wooden craft stick into each rectangle.

**6.** Pour the chocolate melts into a bowl and heat on medium (50%) power in a microwave for about a minute. Stir. If not fully melted, continue to heat and stir at 10-second intervals. Dip the top of each pop into the chocolate and set on wax paper to set.

**NOTE:** Chocolate candy melts, also called coating chocolate, can be found in baking-supply stores or online at www.wilton.com.

# · GIANT CHOCOLATE TREATS ·

*Makes 12 bars*

| | |
|---|---|
| ¼ cup (½ stick) unsalted butter | 6 cups Cocoa Krispies cereal |
| One 10-ounce package marshmallows | 1 cup (6 ounces) chocolate chips |
| | 1 cup chocolate cookies, chopped |

**1.** Spray a 9×13-inch baking pan with cooking spray and set aside.

**2.** Heat the butter in a large nonstick saucepan over low heat until melted. Add the marshmallows and continue cooking, stirring until smooth, 2 to 3 minutes.

**3.** Remove the pan from the heat; add the cereal, chips, and cookies.

**4.** Press the mixture evenly into the prepared pan. Cool completely until set, about 20 minutes, before cutting into 3×3¼-inch bars.

# · TRIX SUPER STARS ·

*Trix are not just for kids in these crowd-pleasing treats.*

---

## Makes approximately fifteen 3-inch treats

¼ cup (½ stick) unsalted butter
One 10-ounce package
   marshmallows

7 cups Trix cereal

**1.** Spray a 9×13-inch baking pan with cooking spray and set aside.

**2.** Heat the butter in a large nonstick saucepan over low heat until melted. Add the marshmallows and continue cooking, stirring until smooth, 2 to 3 minutes.

**3.** Remove the pan from the heat, add the cereal, and stir until well mixed.

**4.** Press the mixture evenly into the prepared pan. Cool completely until set, about 20 minutes.

**5.** Using a 3-inch star-shaped cookie cutter, cut into stars.

TIP
The leftover scraps can be packaged in clear cellophane and tied with ribbon to sell—if the baker doesn't eat them first.

# · MARSHMALLOW MADNESS ·

*Makes 12 bars*

¼ cup (½ stick) unsalted butter
One 10-ounce package
    marshmallows

6 cups Lucky Charms cereal
1 cup mini marshmallows

**1.** Spray a 9×13-inch baking pan with cooking spray and set aside.

**2.** Heat the butter in a large nonstick saucepan over low heat until melted. Add the large marshmallows and continue cooking, stirring until smooth, 2 to 3 minutes.

**3.** Remove the pan from the heat, add the cereal and the mini marshmallows, and stir until well mixed.

**4.** Press the mixture evenly into the prepared pan. Cool completely until set, about 20 minutes, before cutting into 3×3¼-inch bars.

# Two

# A Bounty of Bars, a Surplus of Squares

*Because bars bake in one solid batch and need no frosting, they are the least time-consuming of all bake sale treats. This chapter features twenty-seven of our favorite recipes, from classic Lemon Squares to White Chocolate Caramel Bars. To display the bars, stack them up crisscrossed in tall piles.*

# · SEVEN-LAYER BARS ·

*Probably our single favorite bar cookie ever.*

*Makes 32 bars*

½ cup (1 stick) unsalted butter, melted

1½ cups graham cracker crumbs

1 cup pecans, coarsely chopped

1 cup (6 ounces) semisweet chocolate chips

½ cup butterscotch chips

¾ cup sweetened flaked coconut

¾ cup white chocolate chips

¼ cup peanut butter chips

One 14-ounce can sweetened condensed milk

**1.** Preheat the oven to 325°F.

**2.** Combine the melted butter and the graham cracker crumbs in a large bowl and stir until all of the crumbs are moistened. Pour the mixture into the bottom of an ungreased 9×13-inch baking pan and press firmly into an even layer.

**3.** Sprinkle the pecans evenly over the crumb layer. Sprinkle with the chocolate chips, the butterscotch chips, then the coconut. Next, sprinkle with the white chocolate chips followed by the peanut butter chips. Drizzle the sweetened condensed milk evenly over the entire thing. Press down firmly.

**4.** Bake for 25 to 27 minutes, or until the coconut begins to turn light golden brown. Cool completely in the pan on a wire rack before cutting into bars.

**NOTE:** Bars will keep at room temperature in an airtight container for up to 1 week.

# · TOFFEE BARS ·

*Makes 16 bars*

1 cup (2 sticks) unsalted butter,
   softened
1 cup packed light brown sugar
1 teaspoon vanilla extract
2 cups unbleached all-purpose
   flour

Pinch of salt
1 cup (6 ounces) semisweet
   chocolate chips
1 cup chopped pecans

**1.** Preheat the oven to 350°F. Lightly grease a 9×13-inch baking pan with butter or cooking spray.

**2.** Using an electric mixer on medium speed, cream together the butter, brown sugar, and vanilla in a large bowl until light and fluffy, about 2 minutes. Stir in the flour and salt and mix well. Fold in the chocolate chips and pecans.

**3.** Spread the batter evenly in the prepared pan and bake for 25 to 30 minutes, or until set and golden. Cut into bars while warm. Cool completely in the pan.

# · MR. VERY GOOD BARS ·

*The combination of chips and nuts in these bars is irresistible. Though these are best eaten the day after you bake them, they will keep in an airtight container in the refrigerator for up to 5 days.*

### Makes 16 bars

1⅓ cups unbleached all-purpose flour
1½ teaspoons baking soda
½ teaspoon salt
9 tablespoons (1 stick plus 1 tablespoon) unsalted butter, softened
1¾ cups lightly packed light brown sugar

2 teaspoons vanilla extract
2 large eggs at room temperature, lightly beaten
1 cup (6 ounces) semisweet chocolate chips
½ cup chopped walnuts

**1.** Position one oven rack in the center of the oven. Preheat the oven to 350°F. Lightly grease a 9×13-inch baking pan with butter or cooking spray. Blend the flour, baking soda, and salt in a small bowl and set aside.

**2.** Using an electric mixer on medium speed, cream the butter, brown sugar, and vanilla in a large bowl until light and fluffy, about 2 minutes. Stop the mixer once or twice to scrape the sides of the bowl. Add the eggs and mix on high speed for 5 seconds.

**3.** Add the flour mixture and mix on low speed until almost blended, 8 to 10 seconds, stopping the mixer once to scrape the sides of the bowl. Add the chocolate chips and nuts and mix on low speed for 5 seconds. Spread the batter evenly in the prepared pan.

**4.** Bake on the center oven rack until the top has formed a golden crust, about 30 minutes. Cool in the pan on a wire rack for at least 30 minutes before cutting into bars.

> **TIP**
>
> Because these bars remain very gooey inside (yum!) you may want to transport them to the bake sale in the pan and cut them there.

# · GORP GOODY BARS ·

*These bars look (and are) chock-full of yummy treats. They will easily tempt hungry buyers passing your bake sale table.*

## Makes 20 bars

| | |
|---|---|
| 2 cups bite-size crispy corn cereal squares | 1 cup dried banana chips |
| 2¼ cups thin pretzel sticks, broken in half | ¾ cup golden raisins |
| 1½ cups milk chocolate or peanut chocolate candies | ½ cup (1 stick) unsalted butter or margarine |
| | ¼ cup creamy peanut butter |
| | One 10-ounce bag marshmallows |

**1.** Lightly grease a 9×13-inch baking pan with butter or cooking spray. Combine the cereal, pretzels, candies, banana chips, and raisins in a large bowl. Set aside.

**2.** Melt the butter, peanut butter, and marshmallows in a small saucepan over low heat, stirring until the mixture is smooth. Immediately pour over the cereal mixture, tossing with a wooden spoon until all the ingredients are thoroughly coated. Press lightly into the prepared pan. Let stand until firm, about 30 minutes, then cut into 2½×2¼-inch bars.

# · WHITE CHOCOLATE CARAMEL BARS ·

*Makes 20 bars*

³/₄ cup (1¹/₂ sticks) unsalted butter, melted

2¹/₄ cups packed light brown sugar

1 tablespoon vanilla extract

2 large eggs

2 cups unbleached all-purpose flour

1¹/₂ teaspoons baking powder

1 cup chopped walnuts

1¹/₂ cups (9 ounces) white chocolate chips

**1.** Preheat the oven to 350°F. Lightly grease a 9×13-inch baking pan with butter or cooking spray.

**2.** Using an electric mixer on medium speed or a wooden spoon, beat the butter, brown sugar, vanilla, and eggs in a large bowl until light and creamy.

**3.** Stir in the flour and baking powder until well blended. Stir in the walnuts and 1 cup of the white chocolate chips. Spread the mixture in the pan.

**4.** Bake for 25 to 30 minutes, or until light golden brown and the center is set. Cool completely in the pan. Melt the remaining ¹/₂ cup white chocolate chips and drizzle over the cooled bars. Let stand until the chocolate is set, about 30 minutes, then cut into 2¹/₂×2¹/₄-inch bars.

# · FRUIT-AND-NUT CINNAMON SQUARES ·

*Inspired by Cadbury's Fruit and Nut candy bars, we've substituted cinnamon for chocolate here to create a tasty bar cookie.*

*Makes about thirty-five 2-inch squares*

| | |
|---|---|
| 2 cups unbleached all-purpose flour | ¹/₄ teaspoon salt |
| 1 cup lightly packed light brown sugar | 16 tablespoons (2 sticks) butter, cut into pieces |
| 2 teaspoons cinnamon | 1 large egg, lightly beaten |
| ¹/₄ teaspoon cloves | ³/₄ cup currants |
| ¹/₄ teaspoon nutmeg | ³/₄ cup walnuts, chopped |

**1.** Position one oven rack in the center of the oven. Preheat oven to 350° F. Lightly grease a 10×15-inch baking ban with butter or cooking spray.

**2.** Blend the flour, sugar, and spices in a large bowl. Using an electric mixer at medium speed, beat in the butter, adding a few pieces at a time, until the mixture resembles little peas.

**3.** Add the egg and incorporate with a fork. Stir in the currants and walnuts. The mixture will be crumbly but malleable.

**4.** Turn the batter into the prepared pan and press evenly into all corners.

**5.** Bake on the center oven rack until golden and firm, 20 to 25 minutes. Cool in the pan on a wire rack until warm, then cut into 2-inch squares.

## · RAINBOW BITES ·

*Makes thirty-six 1½-inch squares*

1 cup plus 6 tablespoons unbleached all-purpose flour, divided

1 cup quick-cooking or old-fashioned oats, uncooked

¾ cup firmly packed light brown sugar

½ teaspoon baking soda

¼ teaspoon salt

¾ cup (1½ sticks) unsalted butter, melted

1¾ cups M&M's semisweet chocolate baking bits, divided

1½ cups chopped pecans, divided

One 12-ounce jar caramel ice cream topping

**1.** Preheat the oven to 350°F.

**2.** Combine 1 cup of the flour, the oats, brown sugar, baking soda, and salt in a medium bowl; blend in the melted butter to form a crumbly mixture. Press half the mixture evenly into the bottom of an ungreased 9-inch square cake pan; bake for 10 minutes. Sprinkle the hot crust with 1 cup of the chocolate baking bits and 1 cup of the pecans.

**3.** Blend the remaining 6 tablespoons flour with the caramel topping and pour over the baking bits and pecans.

**4.** Add the remaining ¾ cup baking bits and the remaining ½ cup pecans to the remaining crust mixture; sprinkle over the caramel layer. Bake for 20 to 25 minutes, or until golden brown. Cool completely in the pan, then cut into squares.

> "Why is it that my child will eat any food with colored stuff in it?"
>
> —overheard at a bake sale in Lansing, Michigan

# · OATMEAL CARMELITAS ·

*Makes 20 bars*

| Crust | Filling |
|---|---|
| 2 cups unbleached all-purpose flour | One 12.5-ounce jar caramel ice cream |
| 2 cups quick-cooking rolled oats | topping |
| 1½ cups firmly packed brown sugar | 3 tablespoons unbleached |
| 1 teaspoon baking soda | all-purpose flour |
| ¼ teaspoon salt | 1 cup (6 ounces) semisweet chocolate |
| 1½ cups (3 sticks) unsalted butter, | chips |
| softened | ½ cup chopped walnuts |

**1.** Preheat the oven to 350°F. Lightly grease a 9×13-inch baking pan with butter or cooking spray.

**2.** Lightly spoon the flour into a measuring cup; level off with the back of a knife. In a large bowl, combine all the crust ingredients and, using an electric mixer on low speed, mix until crumbly. Reserve half of the mixture (about 3 cups) for the topping. Press the remaining crust mixture in the bottom of the prepared pan. Bake for 10 minutes.

**3.** Meanwhile, make the filling: Combine the caramel topping and flour in a small bowl; blend well.

**4.** Remove the crust from the oven and sprinkle with the chocolate chips and walnuts. Drizzle evenly with the caramel mixture; sprinkle with the reserved crust mixture.

**5.** Return to the oven; bake for an additional 18 to 22 minutes, or until the crust is golden brown. Cool completely in the pan, at least 1 hour, then refrigerate for 1 to 2 hours, or until the filling is set. Cut into 2½×2¼-inch bars.

# • RASPBERRY COCONUT DREAMS •

*This is a good addition to a bake sale that has too many chocolate offerings.*

## Makes 16 squares

### Crust
1⅓ cups unbleached all-purpose
    flour
⅓ cup granulated sugar
½ teaspoon baking powder
½ cup (1 stick) cold unsalted butter,
    cut into 8 pieces
1 large egg, beaten
⅓ cup raspberry jam

### Topping
1 cup packed light brown sugar
⅔ cup chopped walnuts
¾ cup shredded coconut
2 tablespoons unbleached
    all-purpose flour
1 tablespoon lemon juice
1 teaspoon baking powder
2 large eggs, lightly beaten

**1.** Preheat the oven to 400°F. Lightly grease a 9-inch square cake pan with butter or cooking spray.

**2.** Make the crust: Combine the flour, granulated sugar, and baking powder in a medium bowl. Using a pastry blender or your fingers, cut in the butter until the mixture resembles coarse crumbs. Add the egg; mix thoroughly. Press the mixture evenly into the bottom of the prepared pan.

**3.** Bake the crust for 10 minutes. Spread the jam evenly over the hot crust. Reduce the oven temperature to 350°F.

**4.** Meanwhile, make the topping: Combine the brown sugar, walnuts, coconut, flour, lemon juice, baking powder, and eggs in a medium bowl. Mix well. Spread the mixture evenly over the jam.

**5.** Bake for 20 to 25 minutes longer, or until set and golden. Cool completely in the pan on a wire rack, then cut into 2¼-inch squares.

# · A DATE WITH GINGER ·

*Makes about 18 bars*

| | |
|---|---|
| 1 cup unbleached all-purpose flour | $\frac{1}{4}$ cup chopped candied ginger |
| 1$\frac{1}{2}$ teaspoons baking powder | $\frac{1}{3}$ cup unsalted butter, softened |
| 1 teaspoon ground cinnamon | $\frac{1}{2}$ cup sugar |
| $\frac{1}{4}$ teaspoon salt | 1 large egg |
| $\frac{3}{4}$ cup chopped pitted dates | |

**1.** Preheat the oven to 350°F. Line an 8-inch square pan with parchment paper or aluminum foil; lightly grease the parchment or foil.

**2.** Bring $\frac{1}{2}$ cup water to a boil in a small saucepan over high heat. Combine the flour, baking powder, cinnamon, and salt in a medium bowl; set aside.

**3.** Combine the dates and candied ginger in a small bowl; pour the boiling water over and set aside until soft, about 10 minutes.

**4.** Meanwhile, using an electric mixer on medium speed, beat the butter, sugar, and egg in a large bowl until light and creamy. Stir in the date mixture, then the flour mixture.

**5.** Spread the batter evenly into the prepared pan. Bake for 25 to 30 minutes, or until set and golden. Cool completely in the pan on a wire rack, then cut into bars.

# · MELT-IN-YOUR-MOUTH LEMON SQUARES ·

*Makes about sixteen 2-inch squares*

| Crust | Topping |
|---|---|
| 1 cup unbleached all-purpose flour | 1 cup sugar |
| ¼ cup sugar | 3 tablespoons unbleached |
| ½ cup (1 stick) cold unsalted butter, | all-purpose flour |
| cut into pieces | 3 large eggs |
| | 1½ teaspoons grated lemon zest |
| | ½ cup fresh lemon juice |

**1.** Preheat the oven to 350°F. Lightly grease an 8-inch square cake pan with butter or cooking spray.

**2.** Make the crust: Combine the flour and sugar. Using a pastry blender or your fingers, cut in the butter until the mixture resembles coarse crumbs. Press into the prepared pan and bake for 15 to 20 minutes, or until golden brown.

**3.** Meanwhile, make the topping: Beat the sugar, flour, eggs, and lemon zest and juice in a small bowl just until smooth. Pour over the warm crust. Bake for 25 to 30 minutes longer, or until the topping is set. Cool completely in the pan on a rack, then cut into squares.

# · STRAWBERRY-ALMOND CRUNCH BARS ·

*Makes 24 bars*

| | |
|---|---|
| 1³/₄ cups oats | ¹/₄ teaspoon salt |
| 1 cup unbleached all-purpose flour | ³/₄ cup (1¹/₂ sticks) unsalted butter, |
| or whole wheat flour | melted |
| 1 cup packed light brown sugar | ³/₄ cup strawberry jam |
| 1 teaspoon baking powder | ¹/₂ cup sliced almonds |

**1.** Preheat the oven to 350°F. Lightly grease a 9-inch square cake pan with butter or vegetable oil.

**2.** Combine the oats, flour, brown sugar, baking powder, and salt in a large bowl. Mix well. Stir in the melted butter. Press two-thirds of the oat mixture into the prepared pan. Spread evenly with the jam, then sprinkle the almonds over the jam. Sprinkle with the remaining oat mixture.

**3.** Bake for 25 to 30 minutes, or until golden. Cool completely in the pan on a wire rack, then cut into bars.

# · EVERYTHING PEANUT SQUARES ·

*Makes 20 squares*

| | |
|---|---|
| 2 cups (12 ounces) milk chocolate chips | 1 cup coarsely chopped salted peanuts, divided |
| 1 cup (6 ounces) peanut butter chips | $\frac{1}{4}$ cup smooth peanut butter |
| 1$\frac{1}{4}$ cups sugar | 1 cup marshmallow crème |
| $\frac{1}{3}$ cup unsalted butter | 2 teaspoons vanilla extract |
| $\frac{1}{3}$ cup whole milk | 40 caramels |

**1.** Lightly grease a 9×13-inch baking pan with butter or cooking spray. Heat the chocolate chips and peanut butter chips in a heavy saucepan over very low heat, stirring constantly until the chips are almost melted. Do not overheat. Remove from the heat and stir until smooth. Spread half the mixture evenly in the bottom of the prepared pan. Let stand at room temperature until firm, about 30 minutes.

**2.** Heat the sugar, butter, and milk in a heavy saucepan over medium heat, stirring occasionally, until boiling. Boil for 5 minutes, stirring frequently. Spread the mixture evenly over the chip layer. Sprinkle with $\frac{1}{4}$ cup of the peanuts.

**3.** Heat the peanut butter in a small, heavy saucepan over very low heat, stirring constantly until melted. Remove from the heat. Stir in the marshmallow crème and vanilla until smooth. Spoon the mixture evenly over the peanuts, then top with the remaining $\frac{3}{4}$ cup peanuts.

**4.** Combine the caramels and 2 tablespoons plus 1 teaspoon water in a heavy saucepan over very low heat and stir until smooth. Spread evenly over the peanuts. Spread the remaining half of the chip mixture (reheat if necessary over very low heat, stirring until spreadable) evenly over the caramel. Chill in the pan until firm, at least 45 minutes, then cut into 2$\frac{1}{2}$×2$\frac{1}{4}$-inch (almost) squares.

# · BREAKFAST IN A BAR ·

*With the oatmeal, milk, and OJ baked right in, these bars are a good bet for a morning bake sale. You may even want to list the ingredients.*

## Makes 36 bars (18 bars per pan)

4 cups quick-cooking rolled oats

2 cups unsweetened flaked coconut

1 cup lightly crushed cornflakes

1 cup chopped pitted dates

1 cup golden raisins

$^2/_3$ cup shelled sunflower seeds, toasted

$^1/_2$ cup (1 stick) unsalted butter

One 11-ounce can sweetened condensed milk

$^1/_4$ cup light corn syrup

2 tablespoons frozen orange juice concentrate

**1.** Preheat the oven to 325°F. Lightly grease two 9×13-inch baking pans with butter or cooking spray. Combine the first six ingredients in a large bowl; set aside.

**2.** Melt the butter in a medium saucepan over medium heat. Reduce the heat to low and stir in the condensed milk, corn syrup, and orange juice concentrate until smooth. Slowly pour the butter mixture into the rolled oat mixture, stirring until well combined. (The mixture will be sticky.) Divide and press firmly into the prepared pans. Bake for 20 to 30 minutes until the edges are golden. Cool completely in the pans on wire racks for 5 minutes, then cut into bars.

**TIP**

To toast sunflower seeds, spread in a single layer on an ungreased baking sheet. Bake in a 350°F oven for 5 to 8 minutes, stirring often.

# · JAM-BARRES ·

*Makes 20 bars*

| | |
|---|---|
| 1 cup packed light brown sugar | 1½ cups quick-cooking oats |
| ½ cup (1 stick) unsalted butter, softened | ½ teaspoon salt |
| ⅓ cup shortening | ½ teaspoon baking soda |
| 1¾ cups unbleached all-purpose flour | 1 cup jam or preserves, any flavor |

**1.** Preheat the oven to 400°F.

**2.** Mix the brown sugar, butter, and shortening in a medium bowl. Stir in the remaining ingredients except the jam until crumbly.

**3.** Press half of the oat mixture in an ungreased 9×13-inch baking pan. Spread with jam. Top with the remaining oat mixture, pressing lightly onto the jam. Bake for 25 to 30 minutes, or until golden brown. Let cool in the pan for 15 minutes, then cut into 2½×2¼-inch bars while warm. Transfer the bars to a wire rack to cool completely.

# • CHOCOLATE-GLAZED ORANGE NUT BARS •

*Makes thirty-six 3 × 1-inch bars*

Bars
³/₄ cup confectioners' sugar
¹/₄ cup unsweetened cocoa powder
³/₄ cup (1¹/₂ sticks) unsalted butter,
 softened
1³/₄ cups unbleached all-purpose
 flour, divided
¹/₂ cup orange marmalade
1¹/₂ cups finely chopped pecans,
 toasted and cooled
³/₄ cup packed light brown sugar
1 teaspoon vanilla extract

¹/₂ teaspoon baking powder
¹/₄ teaspoon salt
2 large eggs

Chocolate Glaze
3 tablespoons unsalted butter
1 tablespoon light corn syrup
2 ounces (2 squares) unsweetened
 chocolate
1 cup confectioners' sugar
1 teaspoon vanilla extract

**1.** Preheat the oven to 375°F.

**2.** Stir together the confectioners' sugar, cocoa, and butter in a medium bowl. Add 1¹/₂ cups of the flour and stir to form a crumbly dough. Press the dough into an ungreased 9×13-inch baking pan. Bake for about 10 minutes, or just until the edges begin to pull away from the sides of the pan.

**3.** Spread the marmalade over the dough. Mix the remaining ingredients except the glaze; spread over the marmalade. Bake for 20 to 25 minutes, or until no indentation remains when touched in the center. Cool completely in the pan.

**4.** Meanwhile, make the chocolate glaze: Heat the butter, corn syrup, and chocolate over low heat, stirring until melted; remove from the heat. Stir in the confectioners' sugar and vanilla. Beat in water, 1 teaspoon at a time, just until smooth and of spreading consistency. Spread onto the cooled bars. Let stand at room temperature until the glaze is set, about 20 minutes, then cut into bars.

# · CHEWY CHERRY MAPLE BARS ·

*The dried cherries in this recipe are a nice, chewy surprise. And the hint of maple adds another interesting layer of flavor.*

*Makes sixteen 2-inch squares*

½ cup unbleached all-purpose flour
½ teaspoon baking powder
¼ teaspoon salt
½ teaspoon ground cinnamon
Pinch of nutmeg
¾ cup old-fashioned rolled oats
½ cup chopped walnuts
¼ cup unsalted sunflower seeds

½ cup canola oil
¼ cup firmly packed light brown
    sugar
¼ cup pure maple syrup
1 large egg
1 teaspoon vanilla extract
½ cup dried cherries

**1.** Preheat the oven to 350°F. Spray an 8-inch square baking pan with nonstick cooking spray. Combine the flour, baking powder, salt, cinnamon, and nutmeg in a small bowl; set aside.

**2.** Spread the oats, walnuts, and sunflower seeds in a single layer on a baking sheet and bake, stirring once or twice with a spoon, until they are lightly toasted, 8 to 10 minutes. Remove from the oven and let the mixture cool.

**3.** Combine the canola oil, brown sugar, and maple syrup in a large bowl and stir until smooth. Stir in the egg and vanilla. Stir in the flour mixture until it is just combined, then stir in the cooled oat mixture until well combined. Fold in the dried cherries.

**4.** Pour the batter into the prepared baking pan. Bake the bars until they are golden brown and set, 25 to 30 minutes. Cool completely in the pan on a wire rack, then cut into squares.

**NOTE:** Bars will keep at room temperature in an airtight container for up to 5 days.

# • GRAHAM CRACKER SPECIALS •

*Makes sixteen 2-inch squares*

6 double graham crackers
6 tablespoons unsalted butter
$\frac{1}{4}$ cup firmly packed light brown
   sugar

$\frac{1}{2}$ teaspoon salt
1 cup (6 ounces) milk chocolate
   chips
$\frac{1}{2}$ cup chopped toasted almonds

**1.** Preheat the oven to 375°F. Lightly grease an 8-inch square baking pan with butter or cooking spray.

**2.** Line the bottom of the prepared pan with the graham crackers, breaking them if necessary to cover the bottom completely.

**3.** Combine the butter, brown sugar, and salt in a small saucepan over low heat, stirring until the butter is melted and the sugar has dissolved. Using a small spatula, carefully spread the mixture on the graham crackers so that it covers all of the crackers. Bake until the caramel is bubbling, about 10 minutes.

**4.** Remove from the oven, sprinkle with the chocolate chips, and return to the oven just until the chocolate chips are soft, 1 to 2 minutes. Remove from the oven and use a spatula to smooth the chocolate into an even layer. Sprinkle the nuts over the chocolate. Cool in the pan on a wire rack for 30 minutes, then transfer the pan to the freezer to allow the chocolate to harden, 30 minutes more. Use a sharp knife to cut into squares.

NOTE: Squares will keep at room temperature in an airtight container for up to 5 days.

# • PEANUT BUTTER CHOCOLATE CHEWS •

*Makes 18 squares*

1½ cups chocolate-covered graham
   cracker crumbs (about 17 crackers)
3 tablespoons unsalted butter,
   melted
One 8-ounce package cream cheese,
   softened

½ cup crunchy peanut butter
1 cup confectioners' sugar
2 ounces (2 squares) semisweet
   baking chocolate
1 teaspoon unsalted butter

**1.** Preheat the oven to 350°F.

**2.** Mix the crumbs and melted butter in a small bowl. Press into the bottom of a 9-inch square baking pan and bake for 10 minutes. Let cool completely.

**3.** Using an electric mixer on medium speed, beat the cream cheese, peanut butter, and confectioners' sugar until well blended. Spoon the mixture over the crumb layer, spreading it into an even layer.

**4.** Microwave the chocolate with the butter on medium (50%) power for 1 to 2 minutes, or until the chocolate begins to melt, stirring the chocolate at 30-second intervals. Stir until the chocolate is completely melted. Drizzle it over the cream cheese mixture. Refrigerate for 6 hours or overnight, then cut into squares.

**NOTE:** Squares will keep in an airtight container in the refrigerator for up to 5 days.

# · CHOCOLATE CRUNCHIES ·

*Makes thirty-six 1½-inch squares*

| | |
|---|---|
| 1 cup smooth peanut butter | 3 cups crisp rice cereal |
| ¾ cup honey | 1 cup salted peanuts |
| 1 cup (6 ounces) semisweet chocolate chips | |

**1.** Lightly grease a 9-inch square pan with butter or cooking spray.

**2.** Heat the peanut butter and honey in a heavy saucepan over very low heat, stirring often, until melted. Bring to a gentle boil. Remove from the heat. Add the chocolate chips and stir until smooth.

**3.** Add the cereal and peanuts. Stir until coated. Press firmly in the prepared pan and chill until firm, then cut into squares.

# · PECAN PIE BARS ·

*Though some associate pecan pie with fall, we find these squares
sell well all year round at bake sales. Each square packs in the
flavor of a nice-size slice of pie.*

*Makes sixteen 2-inch squares*

| Crust | Topping |
|---|---|
| 1 cup unbleached all-purpose flour | 2 large eggs |
| ⅓ cup confectioners' sugar | 2 tablespoons (¼ stick) unsalted butter, melted and cooled |
| 2 tablespoons cornstarch | |
| 1 teaspoon salt | ½ cup granulated sugar |
| 7 tablespoons unsalted butter, chilled and cut into 12 pieces | 6 tablespoons light corn syrup |
| | 1 teaspoon vanilla extract |
| | 2 cups pecan halves |

**1.** Preheat the oven to 350°F. Spray an 8-inch square pan with cooking spray and set aside.

**2.** Make the crust: Combine the flour, confectioners' sugar, cornstarch, and salt in a medium bowl. Using an electric mixer, mix on low speed to combine. Add the butter and mix on low speed until the ingredients just begin to come together in clumps. Sprinkle this mixture across the bottom of the prepared pan and press into an even layer. Place in the freezer for 15 minutes, then bake the crust until the edges are just golden, 18 to 20 minutes. When the crust comes out of the oven, reduce the oven temperature to 325°F.

**3.** Meanwhile, make the topping: Whisk together the eggs, butter, granulated sugar, corn syrup, and vanilla. Stir in the pecans.

**4.** Pour the filling over the hot crust and return to the oven. Bake until the filling is just set, 25 to 30 minutes. Transfer the pan to a wire rack and let cool completely.

**5.** Use a sharp chef's knife to cut into squares.

**NOTE:** Bars will keep at room temperature in an airtight container for up to 5 days.

# · WHITE CHOCOLATE SQUARES ·

*Makes 24 squares*

| | |
|---|---|
| 2 cups unbleached all-purpose flour | One 14-ounce can sweetened condensed milk |
| ½ teaspoon baking powder | 1 cup chopped pecans, toasted |
| 2 cups (12 ounces) white chocolate chips, divided | 1 large egg |
| ¼ cup (½ stick) unsalted butter | 1 teaspoon vanilla extract |
| | Confectioners' sugar |

**1.** Preheat the oven to 350°F. Grease a 9×13-inch baking pan. Stir together the flour and baking powder in a small bowl; set aside.

**2.** Combine 1 cup of the white chocolate chips and the butter in a microwave-safe mixing bowl, then heat on medium (50%) power until both are melted, stirring the mixture at 30-second intervals. Stir in the sweetened condensed milk, pecans, egg, vanilla, and the remaining 1 cup chips. Spoon the mixture into the prepared pan.

**3.** Bake for 20 to 25 minutes. Cool completely in the pan. Sprinkle with confectioners' sugar, then cut into squares.

**NOTE:** Squares can be stored covered at room temperature for up to 4 days.

# · HONEY WALNUT WONDERS ·

*Makes 16 bars*

| Crust | Topping |
|---|---|
| 2 cups unbleached all-purpose flour | ²/₃ cup honey |
| ²/₃ cup confectioners' sugar | ¹/₂ cup firmly packed brown sugar |
| ¹/₄ cup cornstarch | ¹/₄ teaspoon salt |
| ¹/₂ teaspoon salt | 6 tablespoons cold unsalted butter, cut into 12 pieces |
| ³/₄ cup (1¹/₂ sticks) unsalted butter, chilled and cut into 12 pieces | 2 tablespoons heavy cream |
| | 3 cups walnut halves |

**1.** Preheat the oven to 350°F. Line a 9×13-inch baking pan with heavy-duty aluminum foil.

**2.** Make the crust: Combine the flour, confectioners' sugar, cornstarch, and salt in a large bowl. Add the butter and mix with an electric mixer on low speed until the ingredients just begin to come together in a ball. Press the mixture into the bottom of the prepared pan with your fingers. Place the crust in the freezer for 15 minutes, then bake the crust until the edges are just golden, 18 to 20 minutes. When the crust comes out of the oven, reduce the oven temperature to 325°F.

**3.** Meanwhile, make the topping: Combine the honey, brown sugar, and salt in a medium saucepan over medium heat. Bring to a simmer, stirring until the sugar dissolves. Let simmer for 2 minutes without stirring. Add the butter and heavy cream and simmer, stirring constantly, for 1 minute. Remove from the heat and stir in the walnuts.

**4.** Pour the hot topping over the warm crust, using the back of a spoon to distribute the nuts evenly. Return the pan to the oven and bake until the topping is light golden brown, 18 to 20 minutes. Cool completely in the pan on a wire rack.

**5.** Invert the pan onto a cutting board; turn the crust right side up. Use a sharp knife to cut into $4\frac{1}{2} \times 1\frac{1}{2}$-inch bars.

**NOTE:** Bars will keep at room temperature in an airtight container for 2 to 3 days.

# · BETTER BUTTER SQUARES ·

*Simplicity itself, and surprisingly delicious.*

*Makes about 25 squares*

| Crust | Topping |
|---|---|
| 1 cup unbleached all-purpose flour | 2 large eggs |
| 2 tablespoons confectioners' sugar, sifted | 1⅓ cups lightly packed brown sugar |
| ⅓ cup cold unsalted butter, cut into chunks | ¼ cup (½ stick) unsalted butter, melted |
| | 1 tablespoon white vinegar |
| | 1 teaspoon vanilla extract |
| | 1 cup raisins |

**1.** Preheat the oven to 350°F. Grease a 9-inch square cake pan with butter or cooking spray.

**2.** Make the crust: Combine the flour, confectioners' sugar, and butter in a food processor fitted with a metal blade and process until crumbly, about 20 seconds. Press into the prepared pan and bake for 10 minutes, or until light golden.

**3.** Meanwhile, make the topping: Combine the eggs, brown sugar, butter, vinegar, and vanilla in a mixing bowl. Stir just until blended, then stir in the raisins. Pour over the warm crust. Bake for 25 to 30 minutes longer, or until set and browned. Cool completely in the pan on a wire rack, then cut into squares.

# · PECAN CHEESECAKE SQUARES ·

*Makes 16 squares*

| Crust | Topping |
|---|---|
| 1 cup unbleached all-purpose flour | One 8-ounce package cream cheese, softened |
| ¼ cup packed light brown sugar | ⅓ cup packed light brown sugar |
| ⅓ cup unsalted butter | 1 large egg |
| | 1 tablespoon whole milk |
| | 1 teaspoon vanilla extract |
| | ⅓ cup finely chopped pecans |

**1.** Preheat the oven to 350°F. Lightly grease an 8-inch square cake pan with butter or cooking spray.

**2.** Make the crust: Combine the flour and brown sugar in a large bowl. Using two knives, a pastry blender, or your fingers, cut in the butter until the mixture resembles coarse crumbs. Press firmly into the bottom of the prepared pan and bake until golden, about 10 minutes.

**3.** Meanwhile, make the topping: Using an electric mixer on medium speed, beat the cream cheese in a large bowl until creamy. Add the brown sugar, egg, milk, and vanilla, beating until smooth, about 2 minutes. Spread the mixture evenly over the warm crust. Sprinkle with the pecans. Bake for 25 to 30 minutes, or until the edges are lightly browned. Cool completely in the pan on a wire rack, then refrigerate for at least 2 hours before cutting into squares.

# • CARAMEL-TOPPED NUT SQUARES •

*Makes about 36 squares*

| Crust | Topping |
|---|---|
| 2 cups unbleached all-purpose flour | 1½ cups (9 ounces) butterscotch chips |
| 1 cup packed brown sugar | ¾ cup corn syrup |
| ¼ teaspoon salt | 3 tablespoons unsalted |
| 1 cup (2 sticks) unsalted butter, | butter |
| softened | 2⅓ cups salted mixed nuts |
| 1 large egg yolk | |

**1.** Preheat the oven to 350°F. Lightly grease a 9×13-inch baking pan with butter or cooking spray.

**2.** Make the crust: Combine the flour, brown sugar, and salt in a large bowl. Using two knives, a pastry blender, or your fingers, cut in the butter until the mixture resembles coarse crumbs. Stir in the egg yolk. Press into the bottom of the prepared pan and bake for 20 to 25 minutes, or until golden. Cool completely in the pan.

**3.** Make the topping: Combine the butterscotch chips, corn syrup, and butter in a small saucepan over low heat, stirring occasionally until smooth and melted. Cool for 10 minutes. Spread over the cooled crust and sprinkle with the nuts, pressing them gently into the topping. Refrigerate until the topping is firm, about 1 hour. Cut into squares.

# Cookies by the Dozen

We could have written a bake sale book with just cookie recipes, but making it only a chapter forced us to pick the best of the best. Cookies go with bake sales like cookies go with…milk! You can price them in bunches—two for a dollar perhaps. Or bake them extra large and charge a premium. A few tips: The old traditions of cookie baking mostly hold up, so it is not lightly that we recommend a newish product that will enhance your baking. But we have to say that the silicone baking mats now on the market (such as the Silpat mat) really improve the process. Cookies never burn, the heat is distributed evenly while they bake, and cleaning the cookie sheet is just about a nonevent. Parchment paper, made of silicone-coated vegetable parchment, is a good second choice. Both are available in kitchen supply shops and some supermarkets.

# · SNICKERDOODLES ·

*These classic cookies are easy and fun to make. Their name alone,*
*on a sign at a bake sale, makes people smile.*

*Makes about 4 dozen cookies*

2¾ cups unbleached all-purpose
    flour
1 teaspoon baking soda
½ teaspoon ground nutmeg
½ cup (1 stick) plus 1 tablespoon
    unsalted butter, softened
1 teaspoon vanilla extract

½ cup firmly packed light brown
    sugar
1 cup plus 1 tablespoon granulated
    sugar
2 large eggs
2 teaspoons ground cinnamon

**1.** Preheat the oven to 350°F. Sift the flour, baking soda, and nutmeg into a medium bowl.

**2.** Combine the butter, vanilla, brown sugar, and 1 cup of the granulated sugar in a large bowl. Using an electric mixer on high speed, beat until light and fluffy. Add the eggs, one at a time, beating on medium speed after each addition. Stir in the flour mixture. Cover the bowl with plastic wrap and refrigerate for 30 minutes.

**3.** Stir together the remaining granulated sugar and the cinnamon in a small bowl.

**4.** Scoop the dough into level tablespoons and roll into balls. Roll the dough balls in the cinnamon sugar, then arrange 3 inches apart on ungreased baking sheets. Bake until the edges are golden, 10 to 12 minutes. Cool on wire racks.

**NOTE:** Snickerdoodles keep up to 2 days in an airtight container. Put sheets of plastic wrap in between the layers until you are ready to display them.

# · HERMITS ·

*An old-fashioned favorite, hermits will fly off the table when priced at two for a dollar.*

## Makes 4½ dozen cookies

| | |
|---|---|
| 3 cups unbleached all-purpose flour | 1 cup (2 sticks) unsalted butter, |
| 1 teaspoon baking powder | softened |
| 1 teaspoon baking soda | 1½ cups firmly packed brown sugar |
| 1 teaspoon ground cinnamon | 3 large eggs, lightly beaten |
| ½ teaspoon ground nutmeg | 1 teaspoon vanilla extract |
| ½ teaspoon salt | 1 cup raisins |
| ¼ teaspoon ground allspice | 1 cup chopped pitted dates |
| ¼ teaspoon ground cloves | ⅔ cup chopped walnuts |

**1.** Preheat the oven to 375°F. Lightly grease three baking sheets with baking spray or butter. Combine the flour, baking powder, baking soda, cinnamon, nutmeg, salt, allspice, and cloves in a medium bowl.

**2.** Using an electric mixer on high speed, cream the butter and brown sugar in a large bowl until light and fluffy. Add the eggs, one at a time, beating well after each addition, then add the vanilla.

**3.** Add the flour mixture to the butter mixture. Stir until well mixed, then stir in the dried fruit and walnuts.

**4.** Using about 1 tablespoon dough for each cookie, drop the dough about 2 inches apart onto the greased baking sheets. Bake for 6 to 8 minutes, or until golden. Let stand on the baking sheets for 5 minutes before removing to wire racks to cool completely.

# · OUR FAVORITE CHOCOLATE CHIP COOKIES ·

*No bake sale is complete without chocolate chip cookies, and we worked extra hard to come up with a recipe that will blow regular CCCs away. We've made these jumbo size, so you can charge a premium for them.*

## Makes about 2 dozen cookies

2½ cups unbleached all-purpose flour
1 teaspoon baking soda
½ teaspoon salt
1 cup (2 sticks) unsalted butter, softened
1 cup sugar

1 cup firmly packed light brown sugar
2 teaspoons vanilla extract
2 large eggs, lightly beaten
2 cups (12 ounces) semisweet chocolate chips
6 ounces (6 squares) milk chocolate, coarsely chopped

**1.** Preheat the oven to 375°F. Combine the flour, baking soda, and salt in a medium bowl and set aside. Using an electric mixer on medium speed, cream the butter, sugar, and brown sugar in a large bowl until light and fluffy. Beat in the vanilla and the eggs, one at a time. Stir in the flour mixture until combined, then stir in the chocolate chips and the milk chocolate chunks.

**2.** Drop the dough by level ¼ cupfuls onto an ungreased baking sheet, spacing them about 2 inches apart.

**3.** Bake for 9 to 11 minutes, or until light golden brown. Cool for 10 minutes on the pan, then transfer to a wire rack to cool completely.

# · OUTRAGEOUS DOUBLE CHOCOLATE CHUNK COOKIES ·

*Makes about 2 dozen cookies*

4 cups (24 ounces) semisweet
  chocolate chips
2½ cups unbleached all-purpose
  flour
1½ teaspoons baking soda
½ teaspoon salt
1 cup (2 sticks) unsalted butter,
  softened

1 cup packed light brown sugar
2 teaspoons vanilla extract
2 large eggs, lightly beaten
1 cup (6 ounces) white chocolate
  chips
1 cup pecan or walnut halves,
  coarsely chopped

**1.** Heat 1½ cups of the chocolate chips in a 1-quart saucepan over low heat, stirring until melted. Set aside and cool to room temperature; do not allow the chocolate to become firm. Combine the flour, baking soda, and salt in a medium bowl.

**2.** Preheat the oven to 350°F. Using an electric mixer on medium speed, beat the butter, brown sugar, and vanilla in a large bowl until light and fluffy. Beat in the eggs and melted chocolate until light and fluffy. Stir in the flour mixture until combined, then stir in the remaining 2½ cups chocolate chips, white chocolate chips, and nuts.

**3.** Scoop out the dough by level ¼ cupfuls and drop 2 to 3 inches apart on an ungreased baking sheet.

**4.** Bake for 12 to 14 minutes, or until set (the centers will appear soft and moist). Cool for 1 to 2 minutes on the baking sheet, then transfer to a wire rack to cool completely.

> TIP
>
> It's important to space these cookies at least 2 inches apart so the heat has ample room to circulate for even baking.

# · WHITE CHOCOLATE MACADAMIA NUT COOKIES ·

*Makes about 6 dozen cookies*

3$\frac{1}{4}$ cups unbleached all-purpose
    flour
1 teaspoon baking soda
1 teaspoon salt
1$\frac{1}{2}$ cups (3 sticks) unsalted butter,
    softened
1$\frac{1}{2}$ cups firmly packed light brown
    sugar

1 cup granulated sugar
2 large eggs
1 teaspoon vanilla extract
12 ounces (12 squares) white
    chocolate, chopped
2 cups coarsely chopped macadamia
    nuts

**1.** Preheat the oven to 350°F. Lightly grease three baking sheets with baking spray or butter. Combine the flour, baking soda, and salt in a medium bowl.

**2.** Using an electric mixer on high speed, beat the butter, sugars, eggs, and vanilla until thoroughly blended. Add the flour mixture to the butter mixture, stirring until thoroughly blended. Stir in the white chocolate and nuts.

**3.** Drop the dough by heaping tablespoonfuls about 2 inches apart on the prepared baking sheets. Bake for 8 to 12 minutes, or until lightly golden. Cool for 5 minutes on the baking sheets, then transfer to a wire rack to cool completely.

> **TIP**
>
> If you have four cookie sheets, bake two sheets at a time, always starting with a cooled sheet. Cookie batter on a hot sheet will spread and cause the cookies to be flatter than intended.

# · JUMBO EVERYTHING COOKIES ·

*These oat-based cookies work best using old-fashioned oats, but the quick-cooking type is a fine substitute. Just avoid "instant" oatmeal, which has a completely different texture.*

*Makes about 2 dozen cookies*

1²/₃ cups unbleached all-purpose flour

1 teaspoon baking soda

¹/₄ teaspoon salt

³/₄ cup granulated sugar

³/₄ cup lightly packed light brown sugar

1 cup (2 sticks) unsalted butter, softened

2 large eggs, lightly beaten

2 teaspoons vanilla extract

2 cups old-fashioned rolled oats

1 cup (6 ounces) mini M&M's

1 cup golden raisins

1 cup (6 ounces) toffee chips

**1.** Preheat the oven to 325°F. Combine the flour, baking soda, and salt in a medium bowl.

**2.** Using an electric mixer on medium speed, cream the sugars and butter until light and fluffy. Add the eggs and vanilla and beat on medium speed until combined.

**3.** Add the flour mixture to the creamed mixture and beat on low speed until combined. Stir in the oats, mini M&M's, raisins, and toffee chips. Drop the dough by ¹/₄ cupfuls onto ungreased baking sheets, spacing about 3 inches apart.

**4.** Bake for 18 to 20 minutes, or until golden brown. Cool on the baking sheets for 5 minutes, then transfer to a wire rack to cool completely.

> **TIP**
>
> Toffee chips, sometimes called toffee bits, can be found near the chocolate chips in the grocery store. You can buy them chocolate-coated or plain; either works in this recipe. Toffee chips freeze well for up to a year, just in case you have leftovers.

# • CHOCOLATE-WALNUT SANDWICH COOKIES •

*Makes about 18 sandwich cookies*

**Cookies**

1 cup walnut halves

$^2/_3$ cup confectioners' sugar, divided

1 cup (2 sticks) unsalted butter, softened

1 teaspoon vanilla extract

$1^3/_4$ cups unbleached all-purpose flour

**Chocolate Filling**

3 ounces (3 squares) milk chocolate, chopped

$^1/_2$ teaspoon vanilla extract

2 tablespoons ($^1/_4$ stick) unsalted butter

2 tablespoons heavy cream

1 cup confectioners' sugar

**1.** Preheat the oven to 350°F.

**2.** Process the walnuts and 2 tablespoons of the confectioners' sugar in a food processor until finely ground; set aside. Using an electric mixer on medium speed, cream the butter and remaining confectioners' sugar until fluffy. Beat in the vanilla. Stir in the flour and $^3/_4$ cup of the walnuts; mix until blended.

**3.** Scoop out the dough by teaspoons and roll into about 36 walnut-size balls. Place 2 inches apart on ungreased cookie sheets. Bake for 10 to 12 minutes, or just until golden around the edges. Transfer to wire racks to cool completely.

**4.** Meanwhile, make the chocolate filling: Combine the chocolate and vanilla in a food processor. Heat the butter and heavy cream in a small saucepan over medium heat; pour over the chocolate mixture. Process until the chocolate is melted, stopping the machine to scrape the sides as needed. With the machine running, gradually add the confectioners' sugar; process until smooth.

**5.** Place generous teaspoonfuls of the filling on the flat side of half the cookies. Top with the remaining cookies, flat side down, forming sandwiches. Roll the chocolate edges of the cookies in the remaining ground walnut mixture.

# • FROSTED CHOCOLATE COOKIES •

*These sweet and simple chocolate cookies are enhanced with a rich chocolate frosting. If you make them large enough—say, 3 inches across—you can probably sell them for over a dollar apiece.*

## Makes 3 to 4 dozen cookies

*Cookies*
1¾ cups unbleached all-purpose
    flour
½ teaspoon baking soda
½ teaspoon salt
1 cup granulated sugar
½ cup (1 stick) unsalted butter,
    softened
1 large egg
2 ounces (2 squares) unsweetened
    chocolate, melted and cooled

⅓ cup buttermilk
1 teaspoon vanilla extract
1 cup chopped nuts (optional)

*Chocolate Frosting*
2 ounces (2 squares) unsweetened
    chocolate
2 tablespoons (¼ stick) unsalted
    butter
About 2 cups confectioners' sugar

**1.** Preheat the oven to 400°F. Combine the flour, baking soda, and salt in a small bowl.

**2.** Stir together the sugar, butter, egg, chocolate, buttermilk, and vanilla in a large bowl. Stir in the flour mixture and the nuts, if desired. Drop the dough by heaping teaspoonfuls (or two for larger cookies) about 2 inches apart onto an ungreased baking sheet.

**3.** Bake for 8 to 10 minutes, or until no indentation marks remain when touched. Immediately remove from the baking sheet to a wire rack to cool completely.

**4.** Meanwhile, make the chocolate frosting: Heat the chocolate and butter in a 1-quart saucepan over low heat, stirring until melted; remove from the heat. Stir in 3 tablespoons water and the confectioners' sugar until smooth.

**5.** When the cookies are completely cooled, frost using 1 to 2 teaspoons frosting for each.

# · SCANDINAVIAN ORANGE COOKIES ·

*Makes about 30 cookies*

½ cup (1 stick) unsalted
  butter, softened
¼ cup sugar
1 large egg
½ teaspoon vanilla
  extract
½ teaspoon orange
  extract

3 tablespoons grated orange
  zest
1½ cups unbleached all-purpose
  flour, plus more for rolling out
  dough
4 ounces (4 squares) semisweet
  chocolate

**1.** Using an electric mixer on medium speed, beat the butter and sugar until light and fluffy. Beat in the egg, vanilla, orange extract, and orange zest until well blended.

**2.** Gradually add the flour while beating on low speed until a soft dough forms, stirring in additional flour, if necessary. Form the dough into a ball; wrap in plastic wrap and refrigerate until firm, at least 1 hour or overnight.

**3.** Preheat the oven to 400°F. Lightly grease two baking sheets with baking spray or butter. Unwrap the dough and place on a lightly floured surface. Roll out the dough with a lightly floured rolling pin to ¼ inch thick, then cut into 2×1-inch bars. Place the bars 2 inches apart on the prepared baking sheets. Gently press the dough scraps together; reroll and cut out more cookies.

**4.** Bake for 10 minutes, or until lightly browned. Transfer to wire racks to cool completely.

**5.** Line the baking sheets with wax paper. Melt the chocolate in a microwave-safe bowl at medium (50%) power for 1½ to 2 minutes, stirring at 30-second intervals. Dip one end of each cookie into the melted chocolate, coating it halfway up the side. Scrape the excess chocolate on the bottom of the cookie back into the bowl.

Transfer the cookies to wax paper and let stand at room temperature 1 hour, or until set.

**NOTE:** These cookies freeze well and can be kept for up to 3 months. Or they will keep for 2 to 3 days when stored between sheets of wax paper in an airtight container and at room temperature.

# • OATMEAL BUTTERSCOTCH DROPS •

*Makes about 4 dozen cookies*

1¾ cups unbleached all-purpose
    flour
½ teaspoon baking soda
¼ teaspoon salt
1 cup (2 sticks) unsalted butter,
    softened
1 cup firmly packed light brown sugar

¼ cup whole milk
1 teaspoon vanilla extract
2 cups old-fashioned rolled oats
1½ cups (9 ounces) butterscotch chips
⅔ cup sweetened flaked
    coconut

**1.** Preheat the oven to 350°F. Lightly grease three baking sheets with baking spray or butter. Combine the flour, baking soda, and salt in a small bowl.

**2.** Using an electric mixer on medium speed, cream the butter, brown sugar, milk, and vanilla until thoroughly blended.

**3.** Gradually add the flour mixture to the butter mixture, beating on low speed until blended. Stir in the oats, butterscotch chips, and coconut.

**4.** Scoop the dough by tablespoonfuls and drop them about 2 inches apart onto the prepared baking sheets. Press flat with a fork dipped in sugar or flour. Bake for 15 to 20 minutes, or until crisp and golden. Cool for 5 minutes on the baking sheets, then transfer to a wire rack to cool completely.

**TIP**

You can substitute peanut butter morsels for the butterscotch morsels with nice results.

# · STOVETOP OATMEAL RAISIN COOKIES ·

*You make this batter on the top of the stove, instead of a mixing bowl.*
*No beaters or bowl to wash!*

*Makes about 3 dozen cookies*

2 cups sugar
½ cup evaporated milk
½ cup (1 stick) unsalted butter
⅓ cup unsweetened cocoa powder
2½ cups quick-cooking oats (not instant)

½ cup chunky peanut butter
½ cup raisins
2 teaspoons vanilla extract

**1.** Lightly grease three baking sheets with baking spray or butter. In a large saucepan combine the sugar, milk, butter, and cocoa. Bring to a boil, stirring frequently. Boil over medium heat for 3 minutes.

**2.** Remove from the heat. Stir in the oats, peanut butter, raisins, and vanilla.

**3.** Scoop out the dough by tablespoonfuls and drop them onto the prepared pans. Let stand until set, about 30 minutes.

# • PEANUT BUTTER-CHOCOLATE CHIP OATMEAL COOKIES •

*Makes about 4 dozen cookies*

1½ cups unbleached all-purpose
    flour
1 teaspoon baking soda
½ teaspoon salt
1 cup (2 sticks) unsalted butter,
    melted and cooled
1 cup firmly packed light brown sugar
½ cup granulated sugar
2 large eggs, lightly beaten

1 teaspoon vanilla extract
3 cups old-fashioned rolled oats (not
    instant)
2 cups (12 ounces) milk chocolate
    morsels
2 cups (12 ounces) peanut butter
    morsels
½ cup coarsely chopped salted
    peanuts

**1.** Preheat the oven to 350°F. Combine the flour, baking soda, and salt in a medium mixing bowl.

**2.** Using an electric mixer on medium speed, beat the butter and sugars in a large bowl until well combined. Add the eggs and vanilla and beat until smooth. Beat in the flour mixture on low speed until just combined. Stir in the oats, chocolate morsels, peanut butter morsels, and peanuts. Cover and refrigerate for 30 minutes.

**4.** Scoop out the dough by heaping tablespoonfuls and drop them about 3 inches apart on an ungreased baking sheet.

**5.** Bake until golden around the edges but still soft on top, 13 to 15 minutes. Cool on the pan for 5 minutes. Using a metal spatula, transfer to a wire rack to cool completely.

**NOTE:** Cookies will keep at room temperature in an airtight container for 2 to 3 days.

# · TRADITIONAL PEANUT BUTTER COOKIES ·

*This is our favorite peanut butter cookie recipe—pure, simple, irresistible.*

## Makes about 5 dozen cookies

2½ cups unbleached all-purpose flour

2 teaspoons baking soda

¼ teaspoon salt

1 cup (2 sticks) unsalted butter, softened

1 cup crunchy peanut butter

1 cup granulated sugar

1 cup packed light brown sugar

2 large eggs

**1.** Preheat the oven to 375°F. Combine the flour, baking soda, and salt in a medium bowl.

**2.** Using an electric mixer on high speed, cream the butter, peanut butter, and sugars until light and creamy. Beat in the eggs, one at a time, mixing well after each addition.

**3.** Add the flour mixture to the creamed mixture, beating on low speed until blended. Scoop the dough out by rounded tablespoons and shape into 1-inch balls. Place the balls on ungreased baking sheets, spacing them 2 inches apart. Press flat with a fork dipped in sugar or flour, making fork marks in both directions.

**4.** Bake for 12 to 15 minutes, or until golden. Cool for 5 minutes on the baking sheets, then transfer to a wire rack to cool completely.

**TIP** For best results bake the cookies on the middle rack of the oven. If you have two sheets, place the second one on the bottom rack. Switch them halfway through the baking.

# • SWEET HONEY OAT DREAMS •

*Makes 18 to 20 cookies*

| | |
|---|---|
| 2 cups unbleached all-purpose flour | ¾ cup (1½ sticks) unsalted butter, softened |
| 1 teaspoon baking soda | ⅔ cup honey |
| ½ teaspoon salt | 3 large egg whites |
| 1½ cups sugar | 4 cups quick-cooking oats |

**1.** Preheat the oven to 350°F. Lightly grease a baking sheet with baking spray or butter. Combine the flour, baking soda, and salt in a medium bowl.

**2.** Using an electric mixer on medium speed, beat the sugar, butter, honey, and egg whites in a large bowl until fluffy. Stir in the flour mixture until combined, then stir in the oats.

**3.** Drop the dough by level ¼ cupfuls onto the prepared pan, spacing them about 3 inches apart. Bake for 11 to 14 minutes, or until the edges are light brown (the centers will be soft). Cool on the pan for 5 to 7 minutes, then transfer to a wire rack to cool completely.

"My son Nick used to like cookies really crunchy. I would let them bake for the whole fourteen minutes. Now he's become a soft-cookie fan: eleven minutes tops."

—Laurie Goldrich Wolf

# · LIME COOLERS ·

**Cookies**

1 cup (2 sticks) unsalted butter, softened

½ cup confectioners' sugar

1¾ cups unbleached all-purpose flour

¼ cup cornstarch

1 tablespoon grated lime zest

1 teaspoon vanilla extract

Granulated sugar, for sprinkling

**Lime Glaze**

½ cup confectioners' sugar

2 teaspoons grated lime zest

4 teaspoons fresh lime juice

**1.** Preheat the oven to 350°F. Using an electric mixer on medium speed, beat the butter and confectioners' sugar in a large bowl until creamy. Add the flour, cornstarch, lime zest, and vanilla and beat on low speed until well blended.

**2.** Scoop out the dough by tablespoons, roll them into 1-inch balls, and place them about 2 inches apart on an ungreased baking sheet. Flatten the balls to ¼ inch thick and sprinkle with granulated sugar.

**3.** Bake for 9 to 11 minutes, or until the edges are light golden brown. Transfer to a wire rack to cool completely.

**4.** Meanwhile, make the lime glaze: Stir together all the ingredients until smooth. Brush the glaze over the cooled cookies and let stand until the glaze is set, about 30 minutes.

# · SUPER CITRUS COOKIES ·

*Makes about 2½ dozen cookies*

½ cup (1 stick) unsalted butter

½ cup sugar, plus more for sprinkling

1 large egg

1½ cups unbleached all-purpose flour, plus more for rolling out dough

1 teaspoon grated lemon zest

1 teaspoon grated orange zest

2 tablespoons freshly squeezed orange juice

1 tablespoon freshly squeezed lemon juice

½ teaspoon baking powder

¼ teaspoon salt

**1.** Using an electric mixer on high speed, beat the butter and sugar in a large bowl until creamy. Beat in the egg until light and fluffy. Stir in the flour, lemon and orange zests and juices, baking powder, and salt. Wrap the dough in plastic wrap and refrigerate for 2 hours, or until firm.

**2.** Preheat the oven to 350°F. Working with one-third at a time, roll out the dough to ¼ inch thick on a well-floured surface. (Keep the remaining dough in the refrigerator.) Cut with a 3-inch round cookie cutter. Transfer to an ungreased baking sheet and sprinkle with sugar.

**3.** Bake 8 to 10 minutes, or until lightly browned on the edges. Cool for 1 minute on the baking sheet, then transfer to wire racks to cool completely.

**TIP**

Our favorite zesting tool is the Microplane grater/zester. It comes in a variety of sizes and can be found in most kitchen stores. The tiny blades are super sharp and make short work of the zesting for these cookies.

# · DOUBLE LEMON BUTTER COOKIES ·

*Makes about 1 dozen cookies*

*Cookies*
2½ cups unbleached all-purpose flour
½ teaspoon baking powder
½ teaspoon salt
1 cup (2 sticks) unsalted butter, softened
¾ cup granulated sugar, plus more
  for bottom of glass

1 large egg
2 tablespoons grated lemon zest, divided
1 teaspoon vanilla extract

*Icing*
1 cup confectioners' sugar
4 to 5 teaspoons fresh lemon juice

**1.** Preheat the oven to 375°F. Combine the flour, baking powder, and salt in a small bowl; set aside.

**2.** Using an electric mixer on medium speed, cream the butter and granulated sugar in a large bowl until light and fluffy. Beat in the egg, 1 tablespoon of the lemon zest, and the vanilla until well blended. Gradually beat in the flour mixture on low speed until blended.

**3.** Scoop out level ¼ cupfuls of the dough and drop them 3 inches apart on two un-greased baking sheets. Dip the bottom of a glass in the additional sugar and use it to flatten the cookies. (Dip the glass in sugar again between each cookie.)

**4.** Bake for 12 to 14 minutes, or until the cookies are just set and the edges are golden brown. Cool on the baking sheets for 2 minutes, then transfer to wire racks to cool completely.

**5.** Meanwhile, make the icing: Combine the confectioners' sugar, lemon juice, and the remaining 1 tablespoon lemon zest in a small bowl; drizzle the mixture over the cooled cookies. Let stand until the icing is set, about 30 minutes.

TIP

If you are in a rush, pop the just-frosted cookies in the fridge—the glaze will set in half the time.

# · CINNAMON YUMMIES ·

*Makes about 4½ dozen cookies*

| | |
|---|---|
| 1¼ cups sugar, divided | ½ cup (1 stick) unsalted butter, |
| 1 teaspoon ground cinnamon | softened |
| 2 cups unbleached all-purpose flour | 1 large egg, lightly beaten |
| ½ teaspoon baking soda | ¾ cup buttermilk |
| ¼ teaspoon salt | 1 teaspoon vanilla extract |

**1.** Preheat the oven to 400°F. Mix ¼ cup of the sugar and the cinnamon in a small bowl and set aside. Combine the flour, baking soda, and salt in a medium bowl.

**2.** Mix the remaining 1 cup sugar, butter, and egg in a large bowl. Stir in the buttermilk and vanilla, then stir in the flour mixture. Drop the dough by rounded spoonfuls about 2 inches apart on an ungreased baking sheet. Sprinkle with the cinnamon-sugar mixture.

**3.** Bake for 8 to 10 minutes, or until set but not brown. Cool on a wire rack.

# • BUTTERSCOTCH SUGAR COOKIES •

*Makes about 4 dozen cookies*

1 cup packed light brown sugar
½ cup (1 stick) unsalted butter, softened
¼ cup solid vegetable shortening
1 teaspoon vanilla extract
2 large eggs, lightly beaten

2½ cups unbleached all-purpose flour, plus more for rolling out dough
1 teaspoon baking powder
1 teaspoon salt
1 cup chopped pecans (optional)

**1.** Combine the brown sugar, butter, shortening, vanilla, and eggs in a large bowl; mix well. Blend in the flour, baking powder, and salt. Stir in the pecans, if desired. Cover and refrigerate for at least 1 hour and up to overnight.

**2.** Preheat the oven to 400°F. Using a lightly floured rolling pin, roll the dough ¼ inch thick on a lightly floured surface. Cut into desired shapes with 3-inch cookie cutters. Place on an ungreased baking sheet.

**3.** Bake for 6 to 8 minutes, or until very light brown. Immediately transfer to a wire rack to cool completely.

# · TRAIL MIX COOKIES ·

*Makes about 4 dozen cookies*

| | |
|---|---|
| 1¹/₂ cups unbleached all-purpose flour | 1 cup smooth peanut butter |
| 1 teaspoon baking soda | 2 teaspoons vanilla extract |
| ¹/₂ teaspoon salt | 3 cups old-fashioned rolled oats |
| ¹/₂ cup (1 stick) unsalted butter, melted and cooled | 1 cup raisins |
| 1 cup firmly packed light brown sugar | 1 cup salted peanuts, coarsely chopped |
| ¹/₂ cup honey | 1 cup (6 ounces) semisweet chocolate chips |
| 2 large eggs, lightly beaten | 1 cup sunflower seeds |

**1.** Preheat the oven to 350°F. Combine the flour, baking soda, and salt in a medium bowl.

**2.** Using an electric mixer on medium speed, beat the butter, brown sugar, and honey in a large bowl until well combined. Add the eggs, peanut butter, and vanilla, and beat on medium speed until smooth. Stir in the flour mixture until just combined, then stir in the oats, raisins, peanuts, chocolate chips, and sunflower seeds. Cover and refrigerate for 30 minutes.

**3.** Scoop out the dough by heaping tablespoons and drop them about 3 inches apart on ungreased baking sheets. Bake until golden around the edges but still soft on top, 12 to 15 minutes. Cool on the baking sheets for 5 minutes. Using a metal spatula, transfer to a wire rack to cool completely.

**NOTE:** Cookies will keep at room temperature in an airtight container for 2 to 3 days.

# · WHOOPIE PIES ·

*Makes about 20 large cookie sandwiches*

| Cookies | Filling |
|---|---|
| 1 cup unsweetened cocoa powder | 6 tablespoons unsalted butter, |
| ½ cup full-fat or low-fat sour cream | softened |
| 1 large egg yolk | ⅔ cup confectioners' sugar |
| 1 teaspoon vanilla extract | 1 tablespoon plus 1 teaspoon light |
| 2 cups unbleached all-purpose flour | corn syrup |
| 1 cup firmly packed light brown sugar | 1 teaspoon vanilla extract |
| 1 teaspoon baking soda | Pinch of salt |
| ½ teaspoon salt | 1 cup marshmallow crème |
| ½ cup (1 stick) unsalted butter, | |
| softened | |

**1.** Preheat the oven to 375°F. Line two baking sheets with parchment paper. Combine the cocoa powder and 1 cup boiling water in a small bowl and stir until smooth. Set aside. Combine the sour cream, egg yolk, and vanilla in a medium bowl and beat lightly with a fork. Set aside.

**2.** Combine the flour, brown sugar, baking soda, and salt in a large bowl; stir to mix. Add the butter. Using an electric mixer on low speed, beat until the butter pieces are no larger than peas. Add the sour cream mixture and mix on low speed until just combined. Add the cocoa mixture and beat on medium speed until combined, stopping the mixer occasionally to scrape down the sides of the bowl.

**3.** Scoop out the dough by tablespoonfuls and place them 3 inches apart on the lined baking sheets. Bake until the tops are cracked, 8 to 9 minutes. Cool on the baking sheets for 5 minutes. Using a metal spatula, transfer the cookies to a wire rack to cool completely.

**4.** Meanwhile, make the filling: Using an electric mixer on low speed, cream the butter and confectioners' sugar in a large bowl until combined. Stir in the corn syrup, vanilla, and salt. Stir in the marshmallow crème. Beat on high speed until light and fluffy, about 3 minutes. Refrigerate until slightly thickened, about 30 minutes.

**5.** Spoon 1 teaspoon of the filling onto the flat side of a cookie. Top with another cookie, flat side down. Repeat with the remaining cookies and filling. Individually wrap cookies in plastic wrap to preserve freshness.

> **TIP**
> Whoopie Pies are best eaten on the day they are made. If you need to make them in advance, keep the cookies and marshmallow mixture separate and assemble just before serving.

# · AWESOME GINGER COOKIES ·

*Make the batter for these cookies the night before you bake them,
as it needs ample chilling time.*

## Makes about 2 dozen cookies

Cookies

²/₃ cup molasses

½ cup (1 stick) unsalted butter,
   softened

¼ cup packed light brown sugar

2½ cups unbleached all-purpose
   flour, plus more for rolling out
   and cutting dough

½ teaspoon salt

½ teaspoon baking soda

½ teaspoon baking powder

½ teaspoon ground cinnamon

¼ teaspoon ground ginger

¼ teaspoon ground cloves

Dash of ground nutmeg

*Confectioners' Sugar Drizzle*

1 cup confectioners' sugar

1 teaspoon vanilla extract

1 to 2 tablespoons whole milk

**1.** Using an electric mixer on medium speed, beat the molasses, butter, and brown sugar in a large bowl until combined. Stir in the remaining cookie ingredients. Cover and refrigerate for about 4 hours, or until firm.

**2.** Preheat the oven to 375°F. Working with half the dough at a time, use a lightly floured rolling pin to roll the dough to ⅛ inch thick on a floured cloth-covered surface. Cut with a 2-inch round cookie cutter dipped in flour. Place about ½ inch apart on an ungreased baking sheet.

**3.** Bake about 8 minutes, or until light brown. Immediately transfer to a wire rack to cool completely.

**4.** Make the confectioners' sugar drizzle: Stir together the confectioners' sugar and vanilla, then gradually add the milk, stirring just until smooth enough to drizzle. Drizzle over the cooled cookies. Let stand until set, about 10 minutes.

# · SOFT MOLASSES DROPS ·

*Makes about 5 dozen cookies*

| | |
|---|---|
| 3½ cups unbleached all-purpose flour | ¾ cup molasses |
| ¾ cup sugar | ¾ cup (1½ sticks) unsalted butter, softened |
| 1 teaspoon ground ginger | 1 large egg, lightly beaten |
| 1 teaspoon ground cinnamon | 1½ teaspoons baking soda |
| ½ teaspoon salt | ½ cup hot milk |

**1.** Preheat the oven to 375°F. Lightly grease baking sheets with baking spray or butter.

**2.** Combine the first eight ingredients, in the order given, in a large bowl and stir to mix.

**3.** Stir the baking soda into the hot milk and add to the flour mixture. Stir until well combined. Scoop out the dough by tablespoons and drop them about 2 inches apart onto the prepared baking sheets.

**4.** Bake for 10 to 12 minutes until dry but still soft. Cool on the baking sheets for 5 minutes, then transfer to a wire rack to cool completely.

# · CLASSIC SHORTBREAD ·

*Amazing but true: just three ingredients make these practically perfect cookies.*

## Makes 36 squares

| | |
|---|---|
| 2 cups unbleached all-purpose flour | 1 cup unsalted butter, cut into |
| ½ cup confectioners' sugar | ½-inch cubes |

**1.** Preheat the oven to 300°F.

**2.** Combine the flour and confectioners' sugar in a large bowl. Using a pastry blender or your fingers, cut in the butter until the mixture resembles fine crumbs. Press the mixture together to form a smooth ball. Press evenly in an ungreased 9-inch square baking pan.

**3.** Prick the entire surface of the dough with a fork through to the bottom of the pan. Bake in the oven for 50 to 60 minutes until just golden. Let stand in the pan on a wire rack for 5 minutes, turn out onto a cutting board, and cut the shortbread into squares while still warm. Transfer the squares to a wire rack to cool completely.

**TIP**

Pricking the dough prevents it from puffing up in odd places. Use the opportunity to make pretty patterns, if you like.

# · ESPRESSO-GLAZED COFFEE COOKIES ·

*Grown-up and special, though known to be a hit with high-schoolers looking for a jolt of sugar and caffeine.*

*Makes about 4½ dozen cookies*

1½ tablespoons plus 1 teaspoon instant coffee powder
½ cup (1 stick) unsalted butter, softened
¼ cup solid vegetable shortening
1 cup granulated sugar
½ cup firmly packed brown sugar
1 large egg
2 cups unbleached all-purpose flour
1 teaspoon baking powder

1 teaspoon ground cinnamon
¼ teaspoon salt

*Espresso Coating*
½ cup sugar
2 teaspoons instant espresso coffee powder

Candy coffee beans for garnish (optional)

**1.** Dissolve 1½ tablespoons instant coffee powder in 1 tablespoon hot water in a large bowl. Add the butter, shortening, sugars, and egg. Using an electric mixer on medium speed, beat until fluffy. Switch the mixer to low speed and beat in the flour, baking powder, the remaining 1 teaspoon coffee, cinnamon, and salt.

**2.** Divide the dough in half and shape each half into a log about 10 inches long. Wrap each roll with plastic wrap and refrigerate for 30 minutes.

**3.** Meanwhile, make the espresso coating: Stir together the sugar and espresso coffee powder on a large plate.

**4.** Roll each log of dough in the coating. Rewrap in plastic wrap and refrigerate for 30 minutes longer.

**5.** Preheat the oven to 375°F. Cut each roll into ³/₈-inch slices. Place the slices about 2 inches apart on an ungreased baking sheet. Sprinkle the remaining coating over the slices. Press a coffee bean into each slice, if using. Bake for 8 to 10 minutes, or until the edges are light brown. Cool slightly on the baking sheet; remove from the baking sheet to a wire rack to cool completely.

# · WALNUT BALLS ·

*These cookies practically melt in your mouth. Display them in a low-rimmed bowl for easy buying and popping.*

---

## *Makes about 3 dozen cookies*

| | |
|---|---|
| ½ cup (1 stick) unsalted butter, at room temperature | 1 cup unbleached all-purpose flour, sifted |
| 2 tablespoons granulated sugar | 1 cup finely chopped walnuts |
| 1 teaspoon vanilla extract | 1 cup confectioners' sugar, sifted |

**1.** Preheat the oven to 300°F. Line two baking sheets with parchment paper.

**2.** Using an electric mixer on medium speed, cream the butter, granulated sugar, and vanilla until light and fluffy. Stop the mixer once or twice to scrape the bowl with a rubber spatula.

**3.** Add the flour and mix on low speed until it is blended in, then stir in the nuts and mix until well blended.

**4.** Scoop out generously rounded teaspoons of dough and roll them into balls. Place the dough balls about 2 inches apart on the prepared baking sheets.

**5.** Bake until just golden, 25 to 30 minutes. To test for doneness, remove one cookie from the sheet and cut it in half. It should appear baked throughout.

**6.** Roll the cookies in the confectioners' sugar while they are still hot, then return to the baking sheets to cool completely.

Don't overbake these; the flavor really suffers.

# · PECAN BITES ·

*These take time to chill, so it's best to bake them a day or two before the sale. Once you taste them you'll likely agree with us that they are worth the time.*

*Makes about 5 dozen cookies*

2 cups unbleached all-purpose flour
$\frac{1}{2}$ teaspoon salt
1 cup pecan pieces, toasted and cooled
1 cup plus 2 tablespoons ($2\frac{1}{4}$ sticks) unsalted butter, softened

$\frac{1}{3}$ cup lightly packed light brown sugar
1 cup granulated sugar, divided
2 teaspoons vanilla extract

**1.** Sift the flour and salt together into a small bowl.

**2.** Place the pecans in a resealable plastic bag. Crush the pecans with a rolling pin or the bottom of a heavy saucepan or skillet until they appear finely chopped; set aside.

**3.** Using an electric mixer on medium speed, cream the butter, brown sugar, $\frac{1}{3}$ cup of the granulated sugar, and the vanilla in a medium bowl until light and fluffy. Add the flour mixture and the pecans; stir until fully incorporated.

**4.** Lay a long (24-inch) piece of wax paper on a work surface. Shape the dough into a rough log 18 to 20 inches in length along one long side of the paper. Roll the log in the wax paper. Refrigerate the dough for 2 hours.

**5.** Remove the log from the refrigerator and roll it on the work surface to round the log. Return the dough to the refrigerator and chill for 30 minutes.

**6.** Preheat the oven to 325°F. Line two baking sheets with parchment paper.

**7.** Unwrap the dough log and cut into $\frac{1}{4}$-inch slices. Dip one side of the slices in the remaining $\frac{2}{3}$ cup granulated sugar and place them, sugar side up, 2 inches apart on the baking sheets. Bake the cookies until just light golden, 12 to 14 minutes. Cool slightly on the baking sheets, then transfer to a wire rack to cool completely.

# Four

## Best Bake Sale Brownies and Blondies

Brownies and their cousins, blondies, are bake sale staples. With the exception of those made with cream cheese, you can bake and then store brownies and blondies at room temperature for up to five days. If possible, bring a knife to your bake sale so that the squares can be cut just before they go on sale. Otherwise cut and wrap them individually in plastic wrap. Obviously, the larger you cut the squares the more you can charge for them. A 3-inch square brownie or blondie is a generous size; try selling them for $2 apiece.

# · ICED CAKEY BROWNIES ·

*Makes 16 brownies*

²/₃ cup unbleached all-purpose flour
½ teaspoon baking powder
½ teaspoon salt
¼ cup (1 stick) unsalted butter
3 ounces (3 squares) unsweetened
  chocolate
1¼ cups sugar

1 teaspoon vanilla extract
4 large eggs
1 recipe Super-Easy Chocolate–
  Cream Cheese Frosting (page 170)
  or one 1-pound can prepared
  frosting

**1.** Preheat the oven to 350°F. Lightly grease a 9-inch square baking pan with butter or vegetable oil. Combine the flour, baking powder, and salt in a small bowl.

**2.** Melt the butter and chocolate in a medium saucepan over low heat, stirring until smooth. Remove from the heat. Add the sugar and vanilla and beat well. Add the eggs, one at a time, beating lightly after each addition. Stir in the flour mixture until just incorporated.

**3.** Pour the batter into the prepared pan. Bake for 25 to 30 minutes, or until set. Cool completely in the pan on a wire rack, then frost and cut into 2-inch squares.

# · SUPER FUDGY BROWNIES ·

*No frosting needed on these chewy squares.*

### Makes 16 brownies

| | |
|---|---|
| 1 cup unbleached all-purpose flour | 2 cups (12 ounces) semisweet |
| $\frac{1}{2}$ teaspoon baking powder | chocolate chips, divided |
| $\frac{1}{8}$ teaspoon salt | 2 eggs |
| $\frac{3}{4}$ cup (1$\frac{1}{2}$ sticks) unsalted butter | 1 teaspoon vanilla extract |
| $\frac{2}{3}$ cup sugar | |

**1.** Preheat the oven to 350°F. Lightly grease a 9-inch square baking pan with butter or vegetable oil.

**2.** Stir together the flour, baking powder, and salt in a small bowl. Heat the butter and sugar in a large microwave-safe bowl for 2 minutes, or until just starting to boil. Stir until mixed. Add 1 cup of the chocolate chips and stir until melted.

**3.** Add the eggs and the vanilla and mix well. Add the flour mixture, mix well, and stir in the remaining chocolate chips.

**4.** Pour the batter into the prepared pan. Bake for 30 minutes, or until a cake tester inserted in the center comes out with moist crumbs. Cool completely in the pan on a wire rack, then cut into 16 squares.

# · MINT BROWNIES ·

*Our favorite from-a-mix brownies, dressed up with peppermint patties.*

---

## Makes 12 to 16 brownies

1 package brownie mix
1 cup chopped chocolate-covered soft mints (such as peppermint patties)
½ cup chocolate chips
½ cup white chocolate chips

**1.** Heat the oven to 350°F. Grease a 9×13-inch pan with butter or vegetable oil.

**2.** Make the batter according to the package directions. Add the remaining ingredients and stir to combine.

**3.** Pour the mixture into the prepared pan and spread evenly with a wooden spatula.

**4.** Bake according to the package directions. Cool completely in the pan before cutting into bars.

# · SNOW-WHITE BROWNIES ·

*White chocolate is not really chocolate at all but, rather, sweetened cocoa butter mixed with vanilla. For some it's too sweet; not for us!*

## Makes 16 brownies

| | |
|---|---|
| $3/4$ cup unbleached all-purpose flour | $1/2$ cup sugar |
| $1/2$ teaspoon baking powder | 2 large eggs, lightly beaten |
| $1/4$ teaspoon salt | 2 teaspoons vanilla extract |
| $1/2$ cup (1 stick) unsalted butter | $3/4$ cup semisweet chocolate chips |
| 4 ounces best-quality white chocolate | $3/4$ cup chopped walnuts |

**1.** Preheat the oven to 350°F. Lightly grease an 8-inch square baking pan with butter or vegetable oil. Combine the flour, baking powder, and salt in a medium bowl.

**2.** Fill the bottom of a double boiler with 1 inch of water and bring to a simmer over medium heat. Combine the butter and white chocolate in the top of the double boiler, making sure that the water doesn't touch the bottom of the bowl. Heat, stirring frequently, until the chocolate and butter are completely melted. Set aside to cool.

**3.** Whisk together the sugar and eggs in a large bowl. Using a wooden spoon, stir in the white chocolate mixture and vanilla, then stir in the flour mixture until just incorporated. Stir in the chocolate chips and walnuts.

**4.** Pour the batter into the prepared pan. Bake for 30 to 35 minutes, or until just set in the centers. Cool completely in the pan on a wire rack, then cut into 16 squares.

# · PEANUT BUTTER SWIRL BROWNIES ·

*Makes 16 brownies*

$^3/_4$ cup unbleached all-purpose flour

$^1/_2$ teaspoon baking powder

$^1/_4$ teaspoon salt

$^1/_2$ cup (1 stick) unsalted butter

3 ounces (3 squares) unsweetened chocolate

1 cup sugar

2 large eggs, lightly beaten

1 teaspoon vanilla extract

$^1/_2$ cup peanuts, or honey-roasted nuts, chopped (optional)

$^1/_2$ cup chunky peanut butter, at room temperature

**1.** Preheat the oven to 350°F. Spray an 8-inch square baking pan with baking spray and set aside. Combine the flour, baking powder, and salt in a small bowl; set aside.

**2.** Fill the bottom of a double boiler with 1 inch of water and bring to a simmer over medium heat. Combine the butter and chocolate in the top of the double boiler, making sure that the water doesn't touch the bottom of the bowl. Heat, stirring occasionally, until the chocolate and butter are completely melted. Set aside to cool.

**3.** Whisk together the sugar and eggs in a large bowl. With a wooden spoon, stir in the chocolate mixture and vanilla, then stir in the flour mixture until just incorporated. Stir in the nuts, if using.

**4.** Pour the batter into the prepared pan. Drop the peanut butter in 10 dollops on top of the batter. Gently run a knife through the batter in several figure-eight patterns to create a marbled appearance. Bake the brownies until they are just set in the center, 25 to 30 minutes. Cool completely in the pan on a wire rack.

**5.** Turn the pan upside down on a cutting board to release the brownies, then turn the brownies right side up and cut into 16 squares.

> ❝Sometimes I toss some peanuts into this batter, or even better, the sweet honey-roasted kind. ❞
>
> —Laura B., East Northport, New York

# · NUTELLA BROWNIES ·

*Toasting the hazelnuts brings out their sweet, rich flavor, and doubles the pleasure of the Nutella, which also has a hazelnut flavor.*

## Makes 16 brownies

$^3/_4$ cup unbleached all-purpose flour
$^1/_2$ teaspoon baking powder
$^1/_4$ teaspoon salt
$1^1/_4$ cups hazelnuts
$^1/_2$ cup (1 stick) unsalted butter
2 ounces (2 squares) unsweetened chocolate, finely chopped

$^1/_4$ cup chocolate-hazelnut spread (Nutella)
$^3/_4$ cup sugar
2 large eggs, lightly beaten
1 teaspoon vanilla extract

**1.** Preheat the oven to 350°F. Spray an 8-inch square baking pan with baking spray and set aside. Combine the flour, baking powder, and salt in a small mixing bowl.

**2.** Spread the hazelnuts in a single layer on an ungreased baking sheet. Bake until just fragrant, about 10 minutes. Remove the nuts from the oven and wrap them in a clean kitchen towel. Let cool for 10 to 15 minutes. Rub the nuts with the towel to remove the skins (it's okay if bits of skin stick to some of the nuts), finely chop, and set aside.

**3.** Fill the bottom of a double boiler with 1 inch of water and bring to a simmer over medium heat. Combine the butter, chocolate, and Nutella in the top of the double boiler, making sure that the water doesn't touch the bottom of the bowl. Heat, whisking occasionally, until the chocolate, Nutella, and butter are completely melted. Set aside to cool slightly.

**4.** Whisk together the sugar and eggs in a large bowl. Using a wooden spoon, stir in the chocolate mixture and vanilla, then stir in the flour mixture until just incorporated. Stir in the chopped hazelnuts.

**5.** Pour the batter into the prepared pan. Bake for 30 to 35 minutes, or until just set in the center. Cool completely in the pan on a wire rack. Turn the pan upside down on a cutting board to release the brownies, then turn the brownies right side up and cut into 16 squares.

**NOTE:** Brownies will keep at room temperature in an airtight container for up to 5 days.

# · MARBLE BROWNIES ·

*Marbleizing is much easier than it seems. Kids love to make the figure-eights in the batter!*

## Makes 16 brownies

| | |
|---|---|
| 1 cup unbleached all-purpose flour | ½ cup (1 stick) unsalted butter |
| 1 teaspoon baking powder | 1 cup firmly packed light brown |
| 1 teaspoon salt |     sugar |
| 1½ ounces (1½ squares) unsweetened | 1 large egg |
|     chocolate | 1 teaspoon vanilla extract |

**1.** Preheat the oven to 350°F. Spray an 8-inch square baking pan with baking spray and set aside. Combine the flour, baking powder, and salt in a small bowl.

**2.** Melt the chocolate in the microwave at medium (50%) power, stirring at 30-second intervals. Set aside to cool slightly.

**3.** Melt the butter in a medium saucepan over low heat. Remove the pan from the heat. Using a wooden spoon, stir in the brown sugar until it is dissolved, then stir in the egg and vanilla. Stir in the flour mixture until just incorporated.

**4.** Pour two-thirds of the brown sugar batter into the prepared pan. Smooth into an even layer with a spatula. Stir the chocolate into the remaining batter. Drop dollops of the chocolate mixture into the pan. Gently run a knife through the batter in several figure-eight patterns to create a marbled appearance. Bake for 25 to 30 minutes, or until just set in the center. Cool completely in the pan on a wire rack.

**5.** Turn the pan upside down on a cutting board to release the brownies, then turn the brownies right side up and cut into 16 squares.

NOTE: Brownies will keep at room temperature in an airtight container for up to 5 days.

# · TRUFFLE BROWNIES ·

*Put a sign up with these saying: Very rich, a small piece will satisfy.*

## Makes 30 brownies

*Brownies*
²⁄₃ cup chopped walnuts
¹⁄₂ cup unbleached all-purpose flour
¹⁄₄ teaspoon ground cinnamon
¹⁄₄ teaspoon salt
6 ounces (6 squares) semisweet
 chocolate
³⁄₄ cup (1¹⁄₂ sticks) unsalted butter
4 large eggs

³⁄₄ cup sugar
2 teaspoons vanilla extract

*Ganache Topping*
6 ounces (6 squares) semisweet
 chocolate
2 tablespoons (¹⁄₄ stick) unsalted
 butter
2 tablespoons heavy cream

**1.** Preheat the oven to 350°F. Lightly grease a 9-inch square baking pan with butter or vegetable oil. Stir together the walnuts, flour, cinnamon, and salt in a small bowl.

**2.** Heat the chocolate and butter in a small saucepan over low heat, stirring until smooth and melted. Remove from the heat; set aside to cool.

**3.** Using an electric mixer on high speed, beat the eggs and sugar in a large bowl until thick, 5 to 7 minutes. Stir in the reserved chocolate mixture and the vanilla. Stir in the flour mixture until just combined.

**4.** Pour the batter into the prepared pan. Bake for 30 to 35 minutes, or until set. Cool completely in the pan on a wire rack, then chill for 1 hour.

**5.** Meanwhile, make the ganache topping: Combine the chocolate, butter, and heavy cream in a small saucepan. Heat over low heat, stirring often, until smooth and melted. Pour over the chilled brownies. Chill until the ganache is set, about 2 hours, then cut into bars.

# · RASPBERRY TRUFFLE BROWNIES ·

*Makes 32 to 36 brownies*

*Brownies*

4 ounces (4 squares) unsweetened
    chocolate
½ cup (1 stick) unsalted butter
2 cups sugar
3 large eggs, lightly beaten
1 teaspoon vanilla extract
1 cup unbleached all-purpose flour
1 cup coarsely chopped toasted
    almonds
¼ cup seedless raspberry jam

*Glaze*

1 cup heavy cream
6 ounces (6 squares) semisweet
    chocolate, finely chopped
2 ounces (2 squares) unsweetened
    chocolate, finely chopped
3 tablespoons seedless raspberry
    jam

Fresh raspberries, for garnish
    (optional)

**1.** Preheat the oven to 350°F. Line a 9×13-inch baking pan with aluminum foil, leaving a 1-inch overhang on the sides of the pan. Lightly grease the foil with butter or vegetable oil.

**2.** Microwave the chocolate and butter in large microwave-safe bowl on medium (50%) power for 2 minutes, or until the butter is melted, stirring at 30-second intervals. Stir until the chocolate is completely melted.

**3.** Stir the sugar into the chocolate mixture until well blended. Mix in the eggs and vanilla. Stir in the flour and nuts until well blended. Spread the batter into the prepared pan, using a spatula to smooth it into an even layer.

**4.** Bake for 30 to 35 minutes, or until a toothpick inserted in the center comes out with fudgy crumbs. (Be careful not to overbake.) Cool completely in the pan. Spread the jam over the cooled brownies.

**5.** Make the glaze: Microwave the heavy cream in a medium microwave-safe bowl on high for 45 seconds, or until simmering. Add the chopped chocolates and jam, and stir until the chocolates are melted and the mixture is smooth. Spread the glaze over the jam on top of the brownies.

**6.** Refrigerate for 1 hour, or until the glaze is set. Using the foil, lift the brownies out of the pan onto a cutting board and cut into bars. Garnish with fresh raspberries, if desired.

# · STRAWBERRY-CREAM CHEESE BROWNIES ·

*Made with fresh berries, these brownies are delicious and elegant.*
*They do require substantial chilling time, so we recommend baking them*
*the day before the bake sale.*

*Makes 16 brownies*

| Brownies | Cheesecake Topping |
|---|---|
| ²/₃ cup unbleached all-purpose flour | One 8-ounce package cream cheese, softened |
| ½ teaspoon baking powder | |
| ¼ teaspoon salt | ¼ cup plus 1 tablespoon sugar |
| ½ cup (1 stick) unsalted butter | 1 large egg |
| 4 ounces (4 squares) unsweetened chocolate | ½ teaspoon vanilla extract |
| | ¼ teaspoon salt |
| 1½ cups sugar | 1 tablespoon unbleached all-purpose flour |
| 2 large eggs | |
| 1 teaspoon vanilla extract | 1½ cups hulled and sliced strawberries |

**1.** Position an oven rack in the lower third of the oven and preheat the oven to 350°F. Lightly grease an 8-inch square baking pan with butter or vegetable oil. Combine the flour, baking powder, and salt in a small bowl; set aside.

**2.** Fill the bottom of a double boiler with 1 inch of water and bring to a simmer over medium heat. Combine the butter and chocolate in the top of the double boiler, making sure that the water doesn't touch the bottom of the bowl. Heat, stirring occasionally, until the chocolate and butter are completely melted. Set aside to cool.

**3.** Whisk together the sugar and eggs in a large bowl. Using a wooden spoon, stir in the chocolate mixture and vanilla, then stir in the flour mixture until just incorporated. Spread the brownie batter in an even layer in the prepared pan.

**4.** Make the cheesecake topping: Combine the cream cheese and ¼ cup of the sugar in a medium bowl. Using an electric mixer on medium-high speed, beat until very smooth. Add the egg and vanilla and beat again until smooth. Stir in the salt and flour.

**5.** Drop the topping mixture by heaping tablespoonfuls over the brownie batter and smooth with a spatula to create an even layer. Sprinkle the berries evenly over the cream cheese. Sprinkle with the remaining 1 tablespoon sugar.

**6.** Bake for 50 to 55 minutes in the lower third of the oven, or until they are set around the edges but still a little wobbly in the center. Cool completely in the pan on a wire rack. Refrigerate until completely chilled, at least 6 hours, then cut into 16 squares.

**NOTE:** These will keep, refrigerated, for 2 days.

# · CHEESECAKE SWIRL BROWNIES ·

*Makes 24 brownies*

3/4 cup (1 1/2 sticks) unsalted butter

2 ounces (2 squares) unsweetened chocolate

2 1/4 cups sugar, divided

4 large eggs

1 3/4 cups unbleached all-purpose flour

One 8-ounce package cream cheese, softened

1 teaspoon vanilla extract

**1.** Preheat the oven to 350°F. Lightly grease a 9×13-inch baking pan with butter or vegetable oil.

**2.** Melt the butter and chocolate in a medium, heavy-duty saucepan over low heat, stirring until smooth. Cool to room temperature. Stir in 1 3/4 cups of the sugar. Beat in 3 eggs; stir in the flour. Pour the batter into the prepared pan.

**3.** Beat together the cream cheese and the remaining 1/2 cup sugar until smooth. Beat in the remaining egg and the vanilla. Pour over the chocolate mixture and run a butter knife through the batter in several figure-eight patterns to create a marbled appearance.

**4.** Bake for 30 to 35 minutes, or until a wooden toothpick inserted near the center comes out slightly sticky. Cool completely in the pan on a wire rack, then cut into bars.

**NOTE:** These will keep, refrigerated, for 2 days.

❝These brownies are great, but I made the mistake of bringing them to an outdoor bake sale on a hot day; they didn't do well in the heat. Next time I'll make sure they are served in an air-conditioned space.❞

—Marty A., Atlanta, Georgia

# · CLASSIC BLONDIES ·

*Rich and chewy, blondies are a pleasant change from brownies. We especially like them made with peanuts, but they're absolutely optional.*

*Makes 24 blondies*

| | |
|---|---|
| 3 cups unbleached all-purpose flour | 1 cup firmly packed light brown sugar |
| 1 tablespoon baking powder | 1 cup granulated sugar |
| 1 teaspoon salt | 4 large eggs |
| 1 cup (2 sticks) unsalted butter, softened | 2 teaspoons vanilla extract |
| | 1 cup peanuts, optional |

**1.** Preheat the oven to 350°F. Lightly grease a 9×13-inch baking pan with butter or vegetable oil. Sift the flour, baking powder, and salt into a small bowl and set aside.

**2.** Combine the butter and sugars in a large bowl. Using an electric mixer on medium speed, beat the mixture until it is light and fluffy, about 3 minutes. Add the eggs and vanilla. Beat on medium speed until the batter is smooth.

**3.** Add the flour mixture to the batter and mix with a wooden spoon until just combined. Stir in the peanuts, if using. Pour the batter into the prepared pan and smooth into an even layer.

**4.** Bake at 350°F for 25 to 30 minutes, or until just set in the center. The blondies will rise during baking and then fall slightly while cooling. Cool completely in the pan before cutting into 24 squares.

# · COFFEE TOFFEE BLONDIES ·

*This recipe has a more sophisticated flavor than a classic blondie. Try them with food-loving adults—they'll sell well and be appreciated.*

## Makes 16 blondies

| | |
|---|---|
| 1 cup unbleached all-purpose flour | 2 teaspoons instant espresso |
| 1 teaspoon baking powder | powder |
| ¼ teaspoon salt | 1 large egg, lightly beaten |
| ½ cup (1 stick) unsalted butter | 1 teaspoon vanilla extract |
| 1 cup firmly packed dark brown sugar | 1 cup chocolate toffee bits |

**1.** Preheat the oven to 350°F. Spray an 8-inch square baking pan with baking spray and set aside. Combine the flour, baking powder, and salt in a small bowl.

**2.** Melt the butter in a medium saucepan over low heat. Remove it from the heat. Using a wooden spoon, stir in the brown sugar until it is dissolved, then stir in the espresso powder until it is dissolved. Quickly whisk in the egg and vanilla. Stir in the flour mixture until just incorporated, then stir in half the toffee bits.

**3.** Pour the batter into the prepared pan and smooth with a spatula into an even layer. Bake for 25 to 30 minutes, or until just set in the center. Immediately scatter the remaining toffee bits over the hot blondies, pressing lightly with the back of a spoon so they stick. Cool completely in the pan on a wire rack, then cut into 16 squares.

**NOTE:** Blondies will keep at room temperature in an airtight container for up to 5 days.

# · OATMEAL BLONDIES ·

*Makes 16 blondies*

1 cup unbleached all-purpose flour
1 teaspoon baking powder
¼ teaspoon salt
½ cup (1 stick) unsalted butter
1 cup firmly packed light brown sugar
½ cup milk
1 large egg, lightly beaten

1 teaspoon vanilla extract
1¼ cups quick-cooking oats or
    old-fashioned rolled oats
¾ cup chopped walnuts (optional)
1 cup (6 ounces) semisweet chocolate
    chips (optional)

**1.** Preheat the oven to 350°F. Spray an 8-inch square baking pan with baking spray and set aside. Combine the flour, baking powder, and salt in a small bowl.

**2.** Melt the butter in a medium saucepan over low heat. Remove it from the heat. Using a wooden spoon, stir in the brown sugar until it is dissolved. Quickly whisk in the milk, egg, and vanilla. Stir in the flour mixture until just incorporated, then stir in the oats. Stir in the walnuts and chocolate chips, if you are using them.

**3.** Pour the batter into the prepared pan and smooth with a spatula. Bake until just set in the center, 25 to 30 minutes. Cool completely in the pan on a wire rack, then cut into 16 squares.

**NOTE:** Oatmeal blondies will keep at room temperature in an airtight container for up to 5 days.

**TIP**
Either old-fashioned or quick-cooking oats works in these tasty treats—just don't use instant oatmeal. Optional nuts and/or chocolate chips can make these a bit fancier.

# · PEANUT BUTTER BLONDIES ·

*Makes 16 blondies*

| | |
|---|---|
| 1½ cups unbleached all-purpose flour | ¾ cup (1½ sticks) unsalted butter |
| 1½ teaspoons baking powder | 1½ cups firmly packed light brown sugar |
| ¼ teaspoon salt | 1 teaspoon vanilla extract |
| 1 large egg | 16 miniature peanut butter cups |
| 1 large egg yolk | |

**1.** Preheat the oven to 350°F. Spray an 8-inch square baking pan with baking spray and set aside. Combine the flour, baking powder, and salt in a small bowl. Combine the whole egg and egg yolk and beat lightly.

**2.** Melt the butter in a medium saucepan over low heat. Remove the pan from the heat and, using a wooden spoon, stir in the brown sugar until it is dissolved. Quickly whisk in the eggs and the vanilla. Stir in the flour mixture until just incorporated.

**3.** Set aside 1 cup batter. Spread the remaining batter in an even layer in the prepared pan. Arrange the peanut butter cups about ½ inch apart on top of the batter in the pan. Using a spatula, smooth the reserved 1 cup batter over the candy.

**4.** Bake for 30 to 35 minutes until just set in the center. Cool completely in the pan on a wire rack, then cut into 16 squares.

"I am not a huge peanut butter fan, but I can't get enough of these blondies. After making three batches for my family, I tried them out for a bake sale. The people who ran the sale all asked me for the recipe—the blondies were definitely a hit."

—Alyssa R., Katonah, New York

# Washing It Down

Drinks are totally optional at a bake sale, and there are pluses and minuses to having them. On the plus side, most people get thirsty when they eat something sweet, so providing drinks is a service. Another plus: You can make a nice profit on beverages. The downside is that drinks aren't low-maintenance: You will need to provide cups, an ice chest, and or a coffeemaker, and you may need to deal with spills. However, if you do go the beverage route we have three recipes that have been winners at past bake sales.

### POWER PUNCH · Makes 30 to 40 servings

A delightful drink for young superheroes.

*2 packages blue-colored Kool-Aid, such as Blue Raspberry*
*    or Blue Berry Yum Yum*
*5 quarts water*
*One 12-ounce can frozen apple juice concentrate*
*One 12-ounce can frozen lemonade concetrate*
*2 liters seltzer*
*½ cup superfine sugar, dissolved in ¼ cup hot water*
*One 5-pound bag ice*

Combine all the ingredients, stir, and serve from a punch bowl.

### SPARKLING STRAWBERRY LIMEADE · Makes 36 servings

*12 cups water*
*4 cups superfine sugar*
*5 cups lime juice*
*3 pints fresh strawberries, washed and hulled*
*12 cups chilled club soda or seltzer*
*Ice (optional)*

1. Bring the water and sugar to a boil, stir, and simmer until the sugar is dissolved. Add the lime juice and cool completely.

2. Puree the strawberries in a blender or food processor. Add to the lime juice mixture, stir, and chill.

3. At the bake sale, fill a punch bowl with the strawberry-lime mixture and the club soda.

4. Serve with the ice, if using.

**TIP:** You can use ready-made lemon- or limeade and begin at step 2.

## • PARTY PUNCH • Makes 30 to 40 servings

*One 46-ounce can cold unsweetened pineapple juice*
*One 46-ounce can cold apple juice*
*One 32-ounce bottle cold cranberry juice*
*Two 28-ounce bottles cold 7UP*

Combine all the ingredients in a large punch bowl. Stir well. Serve cold.

# Five

# Beautiful Breads,
# Marvelous Muffins

As appealing as desserts are, some patrons at a bake sale prefer a less sweet, more healthful snack. That's where quick breads and muffins come in. All the recipes here contain fruits or vegetables (or both!). They're easy to prepare and freeze well if you bake them in advance. Whole loaves sell well (wrap them in cellophane bags tied with curly ribbon) to those looking for a house gift or weekend breakfast treat. Muffins sell well at morning bake sales, especially if coffee is available nearby.

# · APRICOT-PUMPKIN BREAD ·

*This bread feels like autumn, but the ingredients are available all year round, and sometimes it's nice to serve pumpkin flavors when everyone's not sick of pumpkin pie.*

*Makes 2 loaves (24 to 26 slices)*

One 15-ounce can pumpkin (not pumpkin pie filling)
1 cup sugar
³/₄ cup canola oil
3 large eggs, lightly beaten
2¹/₄ cups unbleached all-purpose flour
One 4-serving package instant vanilla pudding mix

1 tablespoon baking powder
¹/₂ teaspoon salt
³/₄ teaspoon ground cinnamon
³/₄ teaspoon ground nutmeg
1¹/₂ cups chopped dried apricots
1¹/₂ cups chopped walnuts

**1.** Preheat the oven to 350°F. Grease and flour two 8×4×2-inch loaf pans; set aside.

**2.** Combine the pumpkin, sugar, oil, and eggs in a large bowl. Combine the flour, pudding mix, baking powder, salt, and spices in a medium bowl. Add the flour mixture to the pumpkin mixture; stir until just moistened (the batter will be quite thick). Stir in the apricots and nuts.

**3.** Spread the batter evenly in the prepared pans, using a spatula to smooth the tops. Bake for 45 to 50 minutes, or until a toothpick inserted in the center comes out clean. Cool in the pans on wire racks for 10 minutes, then remove from the pans to cool completely before slicing.

# · BLUEBERRY-SPICE BREAD ·

*Makes 1 loaf (10 to 12 slices)*

2 cups unbleached all-purpose
   flour
4 tablespoons sugar
3 teaspoons baking powder
½ teaspoon salt
¼ teaspoon ground nutmeg
¼ teaspoon ground allspice
½ teaspoon ground
   cinnamon, divided

¼ teaspoon ground cloves
2 teaspoons grated orange zest
1½ cups fresh or frozen
   blueberries
2 large eggs, lightly beaten
1 cup low-fat milk
3 tablespoons unsalted butter,
   melted

**1.** Preheat the oven to 375°F. Lightly coat a 9×5×2½-inch loaf pan with baking spray.

**2.** Sift the flour, 3 tablespoons of the sugar, the baking powder, salt, nutmeg, allspice, ¼ teaspoon of the cinnamon, and the cloves into a large bowl. Add the orange zest. Measure 1 tablespoon of the mixture and add to the blueberries in a medium bowl. Toss lightly until the blueberries are coated with the flour mixture. (This helps to prevent all the fruit from settling at the bottom of the bread during baking.)

**3.** Whisk together the eggs, milk, and butter in a small bowl until well mixed. Stir the liquid ingredients into the dry ingredients until just moist. Gently stir in the blueberries.

**4.** Spoon the batter into the prepared pan. Stir together the remaining ¼ teaspoon cinnamon and 1 tablespoon sugar and sprinkle over the loaf. Bake for 50 to 60 minutes, or until light golden brown and a wooden toothpick inserted in the center comes out clean.

**5.** Cool in the pan for 10 minutes, then remove from the pan to cool completely before slicing.

TIP

This recipe, like most loaf and quick breads, doubles easily.

# · CRUNCHY BANANA BREAD ·

*Cereal and bananas wrapped up in a muffin—what could be better early in the day?*

*Makes 1 loaf (about 12 slices)*

| | |
|---|---|
| 2 cups whole wheat flour | 1 cup granola |
| 1 cup firmly packed light brown sugar | 2 cups buttermilk |
| 2 teaspoons baking soda | ½ cup mashed banana (about |
| ½ teaspoon salt | 1 medium ripe banana) |
| 1 teaspoon ground cinnamon | ½ cup raisins |

**1.** Preheat the oven to 375°F. Lightly coat a 9×5×2½-inch loaf pan with baking spray.

**2.** Sift the flour, brown sugar, baking soda, salt, and cinnamon into a large bowl. Add the granola and mix thoroughly. Whisk together the buttermilk, banana, and raisins in a small bowl until well mixed. Stir the liquid ingredients into the dry ingredients until just moist.

**3.** Spoon the batter into the loaf pan and bake for 35 to 40 minutes, or until golden brown and a cake tester inserted in the center comes out clean.

**4.** Cool for 10 minutes in the baking pan, then remove from the pan and cool completely before slicing.

# · PECAN PUMPKIN BREAD ·

*Makes 1 loaf ( 10 to 12 slices )*

*Pecan Topping*
⅓ cup firmly packed light brown
    sugar
⅓ cup chopped pecans
1 tablespoon unsalted butter

*Pumpkin Bread*
1⅔ cups packed light brown sugar
⅔ cup canola oil
2 teaspoons vanilla extract

4 large eggs, lightly beaten
One 15-ounce can pumpkin (not
    pumpkin pie filling)
3 cups unbleached all-purpose flour
2 teaspoons baking soda
1 teaspoon ground cinnamon
¾ teaspoon salt
½ teaspoon baking powder
½ teaspoon ground cloves
1 cup raisins or chopped dates

**1.** Preheat the oven to 350°F. Grease only the bottom of a 9×5×3-inch loaf pan with oil.

**2.** Make the pecan topping: Combine all the ingredients in a small bowl and mix until crumbly; set aside.

**3.** Make the pumpkin bread: Combine the brown sugar, oil, vanilla, eggs, and pumpkin in a large bowl. Stir in the remaining ingredients, except the raisins or dates, until well blended. Stir in the raisins or dates. Pour the batter into the pan. Sprinkle with the topping.

**4.** Bake for 1 hour 10 minutes to 1 hour 20 minutes, or until a toothpick inserted in the center comes out clean. Cool for 10 minutes in the pan, then remove from the pan to cool completely before slicing.

# · PRALINE PUMPKIN DATE BREAD ·

*Makes 1 loaf (10 to 12 slices)*

*Praline Topping*

1/3 cup firmly packed light brown sugar

1/3 cup chopped pecans

1 tablespoon unsalted butter

*Pumpkin-Date Bread*

1 2/3 cups sugar

2/3 cup vegetable oil

2 teaspoons vanilla extract

4 large eggs, lightly beaten

One 15-ounce can pumpkin (not pumpkin pie filling)

3 cups unbleached all-purpose flour

2 teaspoons baking soda

1 teaspoon ground cinnamon

3/4 teaspoon salt

1/2 teaspoon baking powder

1/2 teaspoon ground cloves

1 cup chopped pitted dates

**1.** Position the oven rack in the lower third of the oven so that the top of the pan will be in the center of the oven. Preheat the oven to 350°F. Grease the bottom only of a 9×5×3-inch loaf pan with shortening and set aside.

**2.** Make the praline topping: Combine all the ingredients in a small bowl and mix until crumbly; set aside.

**3.** Make the pumpkin date bread: Mix the sugar, oil, vanilla, eggs, and pumpkin in a large bowl. Stir in the remaining ingredients except the dates until well blended. Stir in the dates. Pour the batter into the pan and sprinkle with the praline topping.

**4.** Bake the loaf for 1 hour 10 minutes to 1 hour 20 minutes, or until a toothpick inserted in the center comes out clean. Cool in the pan for 10 minutes. Run a butter knife around the edge of the loaf to loosen it from the pan, then remove from the pan to a wire rack. Cool completely, about 1 hour, before slicing.

# • GLAZED LEMON YOGURT LOAF •

*This moist and yummy cake couldn't be easier to prepare. It will be a big hit with the non-chocoholics at any bake sale.*

*Makes 1 loaf (10 to 12 slices)*

*Loaf*
1¾ cups unbleached all-purpose flour
1 teaspoon baking powder
½ teaspoon baking soda
⅓ cup unsalted butter, melted and cooled
¾ cup granulated sugar
1 teaspoon vanilla extract

2 large eggs, lightly beaten
1 cup lemon yogurt, regular or low-fat

*Lemon Glaze*
¼ cup fresh lemon juice (juice of about 3 lemons)
¼ cup superfine sugar
Grated zest of 1 lemon

**1.** Heat the oven to 350°F. Lightly coat a 9×5×2½-inch loaf pan with baking spray and set aside. Combine the flour, baking powder, and baking soda in a medium bowl.

**2.** Combine the remaining loaf ingredients in a medium bowl. Using an electric mixer on medium speed, beat until smooth. Add the dry ingredients and stir until thoroughly mixed in. Pour the batter into the prepared pan. Bake until a cake tester inserted in the middle comes out clean, 45 to 55 minutes. Let the loaf cool in the pan for 10 minutes before removing it from the pan.

**3.** While the loaf cools, make the lemon glaze: Whisk together all the ingredients in a small bowl. Place the loaf in the container or on the plate you plan to use to transport it. Pour the glaze evenly over the loaf. Let stand about 30 minutes, or until the glaze is set, before slicing.

> **TIP**
> Baking spray is a baker's best friend, especially when it comes to greasing a loaf pan. We prefer it to cooking spray because it includes both oil and flour.

# · LEMON-POPPY SEED BREAD ·

*Makes 1 loaf (10 to 12 slices)*

*Bread*
2 cups cake flour (not self-rising)
2 teaspoons baking powder
1 teaspoon baking soda
$\frac{1}{4}$ teaspoon salt
$\frac{1}{3}$ cup poppy seeds
2 large eggs, lightly beaten
$\frac{3}{4}$ cup sugar
1 cup low-fat lemon yogurt

1 tablespoon grated lemon zest
$\frac{1}{2}$ cup fresh lemon juice
3 tablespoons unsalted butter,
   melted

*Lemon Syrup*
$\frac{1}{3}$ cup fresh lemon juice
$\frac{1}{3}$ cup sugar

**1.** Preheat the oven to 375°F. Lightly coat a 9×5×2½-inch loaf pan with baking spray.

**2.** Sift the flour, baking powder, baking soda, and salt into a large bowl. Add the poppy seeds and blend well. Whisk together the eggs, sugar, yogurt, lemon zest and juice, and butter in a small bowl until well mixed. Stir the liquid ingredients into the dry ingredients until just moist, about 10 strokes. Spoon the batter into the prepared pan. Bake for 40 to 50 minutes, or until golden brown and a toothpick inserted in the center comes out clean.

**3.** Meanwhile, make the lemon syrup: Combine the lemon juice and sugar in a small saucepan over medium heat. Bring to a boil, stirring until the sugar dissolves. Brush the glaze on top of the warm bread.

**4.** Cool for 10 minutes in the pan. Remove from the pan and serve warm or transfer to a wire rack to cool completely before slicing.

# • FIVE-GRAIN CINNAMON BREAD •

*Terrifically moist, this quick bread will make your kitchen smell great while you bake.*

---

### Makes 1 loaf (10 to 12 slices)

$\frac{1}{2}$ cup whole wheat flour

$\frac{1}{2}$ cup unbleached all-purpose flour

$\frac{1}{2}$ cup rye flour

2 teaspoons baking powder

$\frac{1}{2}$ teaspoon baking soda

$\frac{1}{2}$ teaspoon ground cinnamon

$\frac{1}{2}$ teaspoon salt

$\frac{1}{2}$ cup rolled oats

$\frac{1}{2}$ cup oat bran

$\frac{1}{2}$ cup golden raisins

3 large egg whites, lightly beaten

1 cup honey

1 cup sweetened cinnamon applesauce

$\frac{1}{2}$ cup low-fat milk

**1.** Preheat the oven to 375°F. Lightly coat a 9×5×2½-inch loaf pan with baking spray.

**2.** Sift the flours, baking powder, baking soda, cinnamon, and salt into a large bowl. Add the oats, oat bran, and raisins and stir to incorporate thoroughly. Whisk together the egg whites, honey, applesauce, and milk in a small bowl until well mixed. Add the liquid ingredients into the dry ingredients, stirring until just moist. Do not overmix.

**3.** Spoon the batter into the loaf pan and bake for 35 to 40 minutes, or until golden brown and a cake tester inserted in the center comes out clean. Cool for 10 minutes in the pan, then remove from the pan to cool completely before slicing.

# · ORANGE-CHOCOLATE BREAD ·

*The mixture of tastes here is delectable. Double the recipe and keep a loaf for yourself.*

*Makes 1 loaf (10 to 12 slices)*

2 cups unbleached all-purpose flour

1 cup sugar

2 teaspoons baking powder

½ teaspoon baking soda

1 tablespoon unsweetened cocoa
   powder

½ teaspoon salt

2 large eggs, lightly beaten

½ cup plain low-fat yogurt

1 cup frozen orange juice
   concentrate, thawed

2 tablespoons grated orange zest

3 tablespoons unsalted butter,
   melted

1 cup mandarin orange segments,
   drained and chopped

3 tablespoons chopped semisweet
   chocolate

**1.** Preheat the oven to 375°F. Lightly coat a 9×5×2½-inch pan with baking spray.

**2.** Sift the flour, sugar, baking powder, baking soda, cocoa, and salt into a large bowl. Combine the eggs, yogurt, orange juice concentrate, orange zest, and butter in a small bowl and stir until well mixed. Add the liquid ingredients to the dry ingredients and stir until just moist, about 10 strokes. Gently fold in the orange segments. Spoon the batter into the pan and sprinkle with the chopped chocolate. Bake for 40 to 50 minutes, or until golden brown and a toothpick inserted in the center comes out clean.

**3.** Cool for 10 minutes in the baking pan. Remove from the pan and serve warm or transfer to a wire rack to cool completely before slicing.

# · RASPBERRY MUFFINS ·

*Whether you use fresh or frozen fruit, raspberries are always a treat.*

*Makes 12 muffins*

2 cups unbleached all-purpose
  flour
1 cup sugar
1 tablespoon baking powder
½ teaspoon salt
1 cup half-and-half

½ cup unsalted butter, melted
1 teaspoon vanilla extract
2 large eggs, lightly beaten
1 cup fresh or frozen raspberries
  without syrup (do not thaw)

**1.** Preheat the oven to 425°F. Grease the cups of a 12-cup muffin pan or line with baking cups. Combine the flour, sugar, baking powder, and salt in a large bowl; mix well.

**2.** Combine the half-and-half, melted butter, vanilla, and eggs in a small bowl; blend well. Add the mixture to the dry ingredients; stir until the dry ingredients are just moist. Very gently fold in the raspberries. Divide the batter evenly among the muffin cups, filling each cup two-thirds full. Bake for 18 to 23 minutes, or until golden brown. Remove from the pan immediately and cool on a wire rack.

# · APPLE STREUSEL MUFFINS ·

*Makes about 15 muffins*

*Streusel Topping*
⅓ cup granulated sugar
½ teaspoon ground cinnamon
1 tablespoon unsalted butter,
    softened

*Muffins*
2½ cups unbleached all-purpose
    flour
1 teaspoon baking soda

½ teaspoon salt
½ teaspoon ground cinnamon
1⅓ cups packed light brown sugar
⅔ cup canola oil
1 large egg
1 cup buttermilk
1½ cups finely chopped peeled and
    cored apple
1 cup fresh or frozen blueberries

**1.** Preheat the oven to 325°F. Grease 15 cups in two muffin pans or line with baking cups; fill the empty cups with water to help even baking.

**2.** Make the streusel topping: Combine the sugar, cinnamon, and butter, mixing with a fork until crumbly. Set aside.

**3.** Make the muffins: Combine the flour, baking soda, salt, and cinnamon in a small bowl. Stir together the brown sugar, oil, egg, and buttermilk in a large bowl until thoroughly blended. Add the dry ingredients to the liquid ingredients, stirring until just blended. Fold in the apple and blueberries.

**4.** Divide the batter evenly among about 15 cups, filling each cup two-thirds full. Bake for 25 to 30 minutes, or until the tops spring back when lightly touched. Remove the muffins from the pan immediately and cool on a wire rack.

# · PEAR SPICE MUFFINS ·

*Bartlett or Comice are our favorite pears for this recipe, though
any ripe (or slightly overripe) variety will work.*

---

*Makes 12 muffins*

| | |
|---|---|
| 2 cups unbleached all-purpose flour | 1 teaspoon ground cinnamon |
| 1 cup quick-cooking oats | ½ teaspoon ground allspice |
| 1 cup firmly packed light brown sugar | 2 eggs, lightly beaten |
| 1 tablespoon baking powder | 1 cup milk |
| ½ teaspoon salt | 1 cup grated, peeled pear (about |
| ½ cup (1 stick) unsalted butter | 2 medium pears) |

**1.** Preheat the oven to 375°F. Grease the cups of a 12-cup muffin pan or line with baking cups.

**2.** Combine the flour, oats, brown sugar, baking powder, and salt in a mixing bowl. Using a pastry blender or your fingers, cut in the butter until the mixture resembles coarse crumbs. Set aside ¾ cup for the topping; stir the cinnamon and allspice into the reserved topping.

**3.** Stir together the eggs, milk, and grated pear in a small bowl. Add to the dry ingredients all at once, stirring until just moist. Divide the batter evenly among 12 muffin cups, filling each cup two-thirds full. Sprinkle the topping evenly over the batter; pat down gently to make it stick. Bake for 25 to 30 minutes, or until the tops spring back when lightly touched. Remove the muffins from the pan immediately and cool on a wire rack.

# · BEST BANANA MUFFINS ·

*Makes 12 muffins*

1½ cups unbleached all-purpose
    flour
¾ cup sugar
1 teaspoon baking powder
1 teaspoon baking soda

½ teaspoon salt
1 large egg
1½ cups mashed banana (3 or 4 large
    bananas)
½ cup unsalted butter, melted

**1.** Preheat the oven to 375°F. Grease the cups of a 12-cup muffin pan or line with baking cups. Combine the flour, sugar, baking powder, baking soda, and salt in a small bowl.

**2.** Combine the egg, mashed bananas, and melted butter in a large bowl and stir until thoroughly blended.

**3.** Add the flour mixture to the banana mixture and stir until just moist. Divide the batter evenly among 12 muffin cups, filling each cup two-thirds full. Bake for 20 to 25 minutes, or until the tops spring back when lightly touched. Remove the muffins from the pan immediately and cool on a wire rack.

# · CRANBERRY-ORANGE MUFFINS ·

*Makes 12 muffins*

2 cups unbleached all-purpose
    flour
1 teaspoon baking powder
½ teaspoon baking soda
¼ teaspoon salt
½ cup (1 stick) unsalted butter,
    softened
1 cup sugar

2 large eggs
½ cup plain yogurt, regular or
    low-fat
1 tablespoon grated orange zest
½ cup freshly squeezed orange juice
    (the juice of about 2 oranges)
1 cup dried cranberries

**1.** Preheat the oven to 400°F. Lightly coat a 12-cup muffin pan with baking spray or line with baking cups. Combine the flour, baking powder, baking soda, and salt in a small bowl.

**2.** Using an electric mixer on high speed, cream the butter and sugar in a large bowl until light and creamy. Add the eggs, one at a time, beating lightly after each addition. Add the yogurt and orange zest and juice; mix until incorporated.

**3.** Stir the flour mixture into the creamed mixture until just combined. Gently fold in the cranberries. Divide the batter evenly among the muffin cups, filling each cup two-thirds full. Bake for 18 to 23 minutes, or until the tops spring back when lightly touched. Remove the muffins from the pan immediately and cool on a wire rack.

# · CHOCOLATE ZUCCHINI MUFFINS ·

*Make these when zucchini are plentiful in the late summer and early fall. The muffins freeze nicely if you're inclined to bake and save.*

## Makes 12 large muffins

| | |
|---|---|
| 2½ cups unbleached all-purpose flour | ¾ cup (1½ sticks) unsalted butter, softened |
| ½ cup unsweetened cocoa powder, sifted | 2 cups sugar |
| 2½ teaspoons baking powder | 3 large eggs, lightly beaten |
| 1½ teaspoons baking soda | 2 cups shredded zucchini (about 4 medium zucchini) |
| ½ teaspoon salt | ½ cup milk |
| 1 teaspoon ground cinnamon | 1 cup semisweet chocolate chips |

**1.** Preheat the oven to 375°F. Grease the cups of a 12-cup muffin pan or line with baking cups. Combine the flour, cocoa, baking powder, baking soda, salt, and cinnamon in a medium bowl.

**2.** Cream the butter and sugar in a large bowl until light and creamy. Add the eggs, one at a time, beating lightly after each addition.

**3.** Add the flour mixture to the creamed mixture alternately with the zucchini and milk, making two additions of each. Fold in the chocolate chips. Divide the batter evenly among the muffin cups, filling each cup two-thirds full. Bake for 20 to 25 minutes, or until the tops spring back when lightly touched. Remove from the pans immediately and cool on a wire rack.

# · RAISIN DATE BRAN MUFFINS ·

*Makes 12 muffins*

*Date Filling*
1 cup chopped pitted dates
⅓ cup firmly packed light brown
   sugar
1 tablespoon orange juice
1 tablespoon grated orange zest

*Bran Muffins*
1½ cups natural bran
⅔ cup golden raisins

1 cup unbleached all-purpose flour
1 teaspoon baking soda
1 teaspoon salt
½ teaspoon baking powder
1 egg
1 cup buttermilk
½ cup light brown sugar
1 tablespoon canola oil

**1.** Preheat the oven to 375°F. Grease the cups of a 12-cup muffin pan or line with baking cups.

**2.** Make the date filling: Stir together the dates, 1 cup hot water, brown sugar, and orange juice and zest in a saucepan over medium heat. Bring to a simmer and cook until thickened. Remove the pan from the heat and set aside to cool.

**3.** Make the bran muffins: Combine the bran, raisins, flour, baking soda, salt, and baking powder in a large bowl. Combine the egg, buttermilk, brown sugar, and oil in a small bowl; stir until thoroughly blended. Add all at once to the dry ingredients and stir until just moist. Stir in the date filling.

**4.** Divide the batter evenly among 12 muffin cups, filling each cup two-thirds full. Bake for 20 to 25 minutes, or until the tops spring back when lightly touched. Remove from the pan immediately and cool on a wire rack.

# · CHEDDAR-BACON CORN MUFFINS ·

*These savory muffins made with creamed corn are irresistible in the morning.*

## Makes 12 muffins

| | |
|---|---|
| 1 cup unbleached all-purpose flour | 1 large egg, lightly beaten |
| 1 cup yellow cornmeal | One 10-ounce can creamed corn |
| 2 tablespoons sugar | 1 cup grated Cheddar cheese |
| 1 tablespoon baking powder | $\frac{1}{2}$ cup milk |
| $\frac{1}{2}$ teaspoon salt | $\frac{1}{4}$ cup canola oil |
| 6 slices crisp bacon, crumbled | |

**1.** Preheat the oven to 375°F. Grease the cups of a 12-cup muffin pan or line with baking cups.

**2.** Combine the flour, cornmeal, sugar, baking powder, salt, and bacon in a large bowl. Combine the egg, corn, cheese, milk, and canola oil in a medium bowl and stir until thoroughly blended. Add all at once to the dry ingredients. Stir until just moist.

**3.** Divide the batter evenly among the muffin cups, filling each cup two-thirds full. Bake for 15 to 20 minutes, or until the tops spring back when lightly touched. Let cool slightly in the pan.

> "I brought these to an Election Day bake sale and they were sold out by 7:30 A.M.!"
>
> —Madeline C., Saratoga Springs, New York

# Six

# By the Slice

Some cakes and pies can be sold by the slice at a bake sale; others can't. Save your crumbly, gooey, and messy favorites for selling whole or serving at home. The recipes in this chapter are for bake-sale-friendly pies and cakes—they cut cleanly and hold together. When donating a pie or cake, send along a sharp knife, small paper plates, and plastic forks—you'll be a hero. Of course, any of these pies and cakes can be sold whole as well.

## A PIECRUST PRIMER

There are three possibilities for the piecrusts used in this chapter.

- Make it yourself—the best kind! We've provided an easy recipe for a single-crust pie.

- Buy frozen piecrusts in pans. They're very easy, they taste delicious, and all you have to do is pour in the filling. It's a huge time-and-effort saver. Another plus: The disposable pan saves you the trouble of retrieving your pie plate after a sale.

- Get prerolled, refrigerated piecrusts. You'll find these in the refrigerated section of the supermarket. You unroll some; you unfold others; they all taste good and are easy to work with. With these you can use your own pretty pie plate.

You can use any of these crusts for most of the pies in this chapter; homemade is our first choice, but feel free to substitute.

# · SINGLE-CRUST PIE PASTRY ·

*Makes one 9- or 10-inch crust*

| | |
|---|---|
| 1¼ cups unbleached all-purpose flour | ⅓ cup cold solid vegetable shortening, cut into cubes |
| ¼ teaspoon salt | 4 to 5 tablespoons ice water |

**1.** In a medium mixing bowl, combine the flour and salt. Using a pastry blender, cut in the shortening until the pieces are pea size.

**2.** Sprinkle the ice water, 1 tablespoon at a time, over part of the mixture. Gently toss with a fork until all the dough is just moistened. Form the dough into a ball. Chill for at least 30 minutes before rolling out.

**3.** Lightly flour a work surface and a rolling pin. Roll out the dough from the center to the edges into a 12-inch circle. Carefully transfer the pastry into a 9-inch pie plate or 10-inch deep-dish pie plate. Trim the pastry to ½ inch beyond the edge of the plate. Fold under the extra pastry and crimp the edge as desired.

NOTE: If you prefer, you can use two knives instead of a pastry blender.

# · PREMIUM PECAN PIE ·

*One of the all-time favorite flavors, slices of this pie will never be left over at a sale. For an extra treat have a can of whipped cream on hand so buyers can help themselves to a shot.*

*Makes 6 to 8 servings*

1 recipe Single-Crust Pie Pastry (page 137), rolled out and placed in a 10-inch pie plate

1 cup sugar

½ cup plus 2 tablespoons dark corn syrup

6 tablespoons unsalted butter, cut into large pieces

⅛ teaspoon salt

4 large eggs, lightly beaten with a fork, at room temperature

1 teaspoon vanilla extract

1½ cups pecan halves

**1.** Position one rack in the center of the oven. Preheat the oven to 350°F.

**2.** Heat the sugar and corn syrup in a small saucepan over low heat, stirring occasionally, until the sugar is dissolved, about 5 minutes.

**3.** Transfer the mixture to a medium bowl. Stir in the butter and salt; allow the mixture to cool for 8 to 10 minutes, stirring occasionally.

**4.** Stir together the eggs and vanilla and whisk into the cooled sugar mixture, then stir in the pecans. Pour the filling into the pie shell.

**5.** Bake in the center of the oven for 50 to 60 minutes, or until the top is fully risen, set, and crisp to the touch. Let stand at room temperature for at least 1 hour. Refrigerate until ready to slice and serve.

**NOTE:** This pie can be made 1 day ahead and refrigerated.

# · CHOCOLATE-BOURBON PECAN PIE ·

*Not for school bake sales!*

---

## Makes 12 to 14 slices

1 recipe Single-Crust Pie Pastry
(page 137), rolled out and placed in
a 10-inch pie plate

4 ounces (4 squares) unsweetened
chocolate

1 cup sugar

³/₄ cup dark corn syrup

¹/₄ cup (¹/₂ stick) unsalted butter, at
room temperature

¹/₄ teaspoon salt

4 large eggs, lightly beaten, at room
temperature

¹/₄ cup bourbon

2 teaspoons vanilla extract

1¹/₄ cups pecan halves

**1.** Position one rack in the center of the oven. Preheat the oven to 350°F.

**2.** Fill the bottom of a double boiler with 1 inch of water and bring to a simmer over medium heat. Add the chocolate and stir to melt. Set aside.

**3.** Heat the sugar and corn syrup in a small saucepan over low heat, stirring occasionally, until the sugar is dissolved, about 5 minutes. Transfer the mixture to a medium bowl.

**4.** Stir in the butter and salt and allow the mixture to cool for 8 to 10 minutes, stirring occasionally. Stir together the eggs and bourbon, then whisk into the mixture.

**5.** Add the melted chocolate and the vanilla and whisk vigorously until blended. Stir in the pecans. Pour the filling into the pie shell.

**6.** Bake in the center of the oven for 55 to 60 minutes, or until the top is risen, set, and crisp to the touch. Remove the pie from the oven and cool it completely on a rack.

# · CHOCOLATE CHIP PIE ·

*This pie is perfect for someone who likes a chewy cookie; with a slice you get a high proportion of soft insides. It's also a hit with middle school and high school kids who are hard to wow with straightforward chocolate chip cookies.*

## Makes 8 servings

1 recipe Single-Crust Pie Pastry (page 137), rolled out and placed in a 9-inch pie plate

$\frac{1}{2}$ cup unbleached all-purpose flour

1 cup sugar

2 large eggs, lightly beaten

$\frac{1}{4}$ cup ($\frac{1}{2}$ stick) unsalted butter, melted and cooled

2 teaspoons vanilla extract

1 cup (6 ounces) semisweet chocolate chips

1 cup walnuts, chopped (optional)

**1.** Preheat the oven to 325°F.

**2.** In a large bowl, stir together the flour and sugar. Add the eggs, one at a time, stirring after each addition. Add the remaining ingredients and stir until thoroughly mixed.

**3.** Pour the mixture into the pie shell and bake until the center stays set when gently shaken, about 1 hour. Cool completely before slicing.

**TIP**

Two delicious variations: Substitute peanut butter chips for the chocolate chips. Add 1/2 cup raisins when you stir in the nuts.

# · PUMPKIN-HONEY PIE ·

*Slightly fancier than plain pumpkin, this pie is a hit all through the autumn months. It should be chilled before bringing it to the bake sale, but will be fine at room temperature for several hours.*

## Makes 8 slices

1 recipe Single-Crust Pie Pastry
  (page 137)
3 large eggs, lightly beaten
2 cups mashed cooked pumpkin or
  one 16-ounce can pumpkin puree
  (not pumpkin pie filling)
$3/4$ cup honey
$1/2$ cup milk
$1/4$ cup heavy cream
$1 1/2$ teaspoons ground cinnamon
$1/2$ teaspoon salt
$1/4$ teaspoon ground ginger
$1/2$ teaspoon ground nutmeg
8 decorative candies, such as candy
  corn or candy pumpkins
  (optional)

**1.** Preheat the oven to 400°F.

**2.** Combine all the ingredients except the candies in a large bowl. Using a whisk or rotary beater, mix until smooth. Pour the filling into the pie shell.

**3.** Cover the crust edges with a 2- to 3-inch strip of aluminum foil to prevent excessive browning; remove the foil during the last 15 minutes of baking.

**4.** Bake for 50 to 55 minutes, or until a knife inserted 1 inch from the edge comes out clean. Place on a rack to cool. If using the candies, space them evenly around the pie, about 2 inches in from the crust edge. Cool for 15 minutes; refrigerate until chilled.

> **TIP**
> We recommend spacing the candies evenly around the pie to make it easy to slice into even pieces at the bake sale.

# · SWEET POTATO PIE ·

*This is an inexpensive pie to bake. If you want to make it on the day of a bake sale, it can be served warm. If you make it the day before, you can store it, covered, at room temperature and serve it at room temperature.*

### Makes 8 slices

1 recipe Single-Crust Pie Pastry
   (page 137)
2 medium sweet potatoes, peeled and
   cubed
¼ cup (½ stick) unsalted butter,
   softened

1 cup packed light brown sugar
1 teaspoon ground cinnamon
¼ teaspoon ground nutmeg
3 large eggs, lightly beaten
One 12-ounce can evaporated milk

**1.** Preheat the oven to 450°F.

**2.** Place the sweet potatoes in a medium saucepan and fill with water to cover. Bring to a boil over medium-high heat. Boil for 15 minutes, or until fork-tender. Drain well and set aside to cool.

**3.** Line the pie shell with a double thickness of aluminum foil. Bake for 8 minutes. Remove the foil; bake for 4 to 5 minutes longer. Set on a rack to cool. Reduce the oven temperature to 400°F.

**4.** Combine the cooked potatoes and the butter in a large bowl. Using an electric mixer on high speed, beat until smooth. Add the brown sugar, cinnamon, and nutmeg and beat until combined. Add the eggs and beat on low speed until just combined. Stir in the milk.

**5.** Pour the filling into the crust. Cover the edge of the pie with a 2- to 3-inch strip of foil to prevent excessive browning; remove the foil during the last 15 minutes of baking. Bake at 400°F for 10 minutes. Reduce the oven temperature to 350°F. Bake for 40 to 50 minutes, or until a knife inserted in the center comes out clean. Cool on a rack for 1 hour.

# · SHAKER SUGAR PIE ·

*Makes 12 slices*

1 recipe Single-Crust Pie Pastry (page 137), rolled out and placed in a 9-inch pie plate, or 1 frozen piecrust
1 cup packed light brown sugar
½ cup (1 stick) unsalted butter, softened
2 tablespoons unbleached all-purpose flour
1½ cups heavy cream
1 teaspoon vanilla extract
1 large egg
Freshly ground nutmeg

**1.** Preheat the oven to 450°F.

**2.** Mix the brown sugar, butter, and flour in a small bowl until well blended; spread in the bottom of the pie shell.

**3.** Using an electric mixer on medium speed, beat the heavy cream, vanilla, and egg until well blended. Pour over the brown sugar mixture. Sprinkle with nutmeg.

**4.** Bake for 10 minutes. Reduce the oven temperature to 350°F. Bake for 25 to 30 minutes longer, or until a knife inserted in the center comes out clean. Cool for at least 1 hour at room temperature; refrigerate until serving.

# · PINEAPPLE UPSIDE-DOWN CAKE ·

*Upside-down cakes were originally called skillet cakes, cooked in cast-iron pans on top of the stove. This wonderful old-fashioned cake made with caramelized fruit seems to be having a comeback—it's the height of cake comfort food.*

*Makes sixteen 2-inch squares*

Topping
3/4 cup lightly packed light brown
   sugar
1/2 teaspoon salt
3 tablespoons unsalted butter, melted
1 1/2 cans (20 ounces each) pineapple
   chunks, drained completely

Cake
1 cup unbleached all-purpose flour
1/2 teaspoon baking soda

1/2 teaspoon baking powder
1/4 teaspoon salt
6 tablespoons unsalted butter,
   softened
1 cup granulated sugar, divided
2 teaspoons vanilla extract
2 large eggs, separated, at room
   temperature
1/2 cup buttermilk

**1.** Position one oven rack just below the center of the oven. Preheat the oven to 350°F.

**2.** Make the topping: Combine the brown sugar, salt, and butter in a medium bowl. Add the pineapple and stir to combine. Spread the topping evenly in an 8-inch square pan and set aside.

**3.** Make the cake: Sift the flour, baking soda, baking powder, and salt together into a small bowl.

**4.** Using an electric mixer on medium speed, cream the butter, 3/4 cup of the granulated sugar, and the vanilla in a medium bowl until light and fluffy, stopping the mixer once or twice to scrape the sides of the bowl with a rubber spatula. Add the egg yolks and beat on low speed until they are incorporated.

**5.** With the mixer on low speed, add half the dry ingredients to the butter mixture and blend until incorporated. Scrape the bowl. Add the buttermilk and mix on low speed. Scrape the bowl. Fold in the rest of the dry ingredients by hand, scraping the sides of the bowl.

**6.** Clean the beaters thoroughly. Using an electric mixer on medium-high speed, beat the egg whites until frothy. With the mixer running gradually, add the remaining $\frac{1}{4}$ cup sugar and continue beating the whites until they form soft peaks.

**7.** Stir one-third of the whites into the batter with a wooden spoon, then fold in the remaining whites with a rubber spatula.

**8.** Spread the batter evenly over the topping and place the pan on a rack in the oven just below the center. Bake for about 50 minutes, or until the top is golden and springs back to the touch, and a tester inserted in the center comes out dry.

**9.** Let the cake cool in the pan on a wire rack for about 2 hours. Run a metal spatula or butter knife around the sides of the pan. Place a plate upside down on top of the pan. Holding the edges of the pan on the plate, turn the plate right side up and carefully lift the pan off the cake. Cut into squares just before bringing to the bake sale.

**NOTE:** This cake will keep for several days stored at room temperature in a cake saver.

# · FROSTED BANANA CAKE ·

*An all-age favorite, especially with Banana Buttercream Frosting.*

*Makes about 12 slices*

*Banana Cake*
2 cups unbleached all-purpose flour
1³/₄ teaspoons baking powder
1 teaspoon baking soda
¹/₂ teaspoon salt
1¹/₄ cups granulated sugar
1 cup mashed ripe banana (about
   2 medium bananas)
¹/₂ cup (1 stick) unsalted butter, softened
¹/₂ cup buttermilk

2 large eggs, lightly beaten
2 teaspoons vanilla extract

*Banana Buttercream Frosting*
¹/₂ cup (1 stick) butter, softened
¹/₂ cup mashed ripe banana (about
   1 medium bananas)
4 cups confectioners' sugar, sifted
1 tablespoon half-and-half
1 teaspoon vanilla extract

**1.** Preheat the oven to 350°F. Grease and flour two 8-inch round cake pans.

**2.** Combine the flour, baking powder, baking soda, and salt in a large bowl; stir to mix. Add the sugar, mashed bananas, butter, and buttermilk. Using an electric mixer on medium speed, beat for 2 minutes. Add the eggs and vanilla and beat for 1 minute. Spread the batter evenly into the prepared pans, smoothing the tops with a rubber spatula.

**3.** Bake for 35 to 40 minutes, or until a toothpick inserted in the center comes out clean. Cool for 10 minutes in the pans on a wire rack, then remove the layers from the pans and cool completely on a wire rack before frosting.

**4.** Meanwhile, make the banana buttercream frosting: Using an electric mixer on medium speed, cream the butter, mashed banana, and half of the confectioners' sugar until creamy. Add the half-and-half and vanilla and beat until combined. With the mixer running, add the remaining confectioners' sugar, beating until smooth and creamy.

**5.** Frost the top of one cooled layer, then stack the second layer on top. Frost the sides then the top of the cake, and store in a cake saver or loosely covered container.

# · APPLE SPICE CAKE ·

*This is an easy recipe for children to help bake, especially if they like to measure ingredients. It's also a good one to make well in advance of a bake sale, as it will stay moist for 4 to 5 days when tightly wrapped.*

*Makes 14 to 16 slices*

Cake
3 cups unbleached all-purpose flour
2 teaspoons ground cinnamon
$\frac{1}{2}$ teaspoon ground nutmeg
$\frac{1}{4}$ teaspoon ground cloves
1 teaspoon baking soda
$\frac{1}{2}$ teaspoon salt
1 cup (2 sticks) unsalted butter,
    at room temperature
$\frac{1}{4}$ cup canola oil
2 cups granulated sugar

2 teaspoons vanilla extract
3 large eggs, at room temperature
4 cups apples (3 to 4 large apples),
    peeled, cored, and cut into $\frac{1}{2}$-inch
    cubes
$\frac{1}{2}$ cup golden raisins

Topping
1 teaspoon cinnamon
1 tablespoon brown sugar

**1.** Position one oven rack in the center of the oven. Preheat the oven to 350°F. Lightly grease a 10-inch tube pan with a removable bottom. Sift together the flour, spices, baking soda, and salt into a small bowl.

**2.** Using an electric mixer on medium speed, cream the butter, oil, sugar, and vanilla in a medium bowl until blended, stopping to scrape down the sides of the bowl.

**3.** Add the eggs, one at a time, mixing on medium speed after each addition until blended, scraping the bowl each time. After all the eggs are added, mix again for 10 seconds. Add half the dry ingredients and blend on low speed for 15 seconds. Scrape the bowl, add the rest of the dry ingredients, and mix on low speed until blended, about 5 seconds more.

**4.** Using a wooden spoon, fold in the apples and raisins. Pour the batter into the pan, using a rubber spatula to scrape the sides.

**5.** Make the topping: Stir together the cinnamon and brown sugar, then sprinkle over the batter. Bake in the center of the oven for about 1 hour, or until the top is firm and golden and a tester inserted at the cake's highest point comes out clean. Let cool in the pan for 15 minutes, then turn the cake out onto a wire rack to cool completely. Store at room temperature wrapped in aluminum foil.

# · SILKY PECAN COFFEE CAKE ·

*This cake is an annual favorite at Election Day bake sales. It will stay moist all day long as voters turn out at the polls.*

## Makes 8 to 10 slices

**Cake**

1 cup sour cream

1 teaspoon baking soda

1/2 cup (1 stick) unsalted butter, softened

1 cup granulated sugar

2 large eggs, lightly beaten

2 teaspoons vanilla extract

1 3/4 cups unbleached all-purpose flour

1 teaspoon baking powder

1/4 teaspoon salt

**Topping**

1/2 cup packed light brown sugar

1/3 cup chopped pecans

1 teaspoon ground cinnamon

**1.** Preheat the oven to 350°F. Lightly grease a 9-inch springform pan with baking spray.

**2.** Stir together the sour cream and baking soda in a small bowl; set aside.

**3.** Using an electric mixer on medium speed, cream the butter and sugar until light and fluffy. Add the eggs, one at a time, beating thoroughly after each addition. Stir in the vanilla.

**4.** Combine the flour, baking powder, and salt. Using an electric mixer on low speed, mix one-third of the flour mixture into the creamed mixture. Mix in half of the sour cream mixture, then repeat with the remaining two-thirds of the dry ingredients and the remaining half of the sour cream mixture, ending with the dry ingredients. Spread half of the batter into the prepared pan.

**5.** Make the topping: Combine the brown sugar, pecans, and cinnamon. Sprinkle half of the mixture over the batter in the pan. Cover with the remaining batter, then the remaining topping. Press the topping gently into the batter.

**6.** Bake for 45 to 50 minutes, or until a toothpick inserted in the center comes out clean. (Check the cake halfway through the baking time and cover with aluminum foil if the top is browning too quickly.) Cool completely in the pan on a rack. Loosen the edge of the cake with a knife, then remove the ring from the pan.

**7.** Wrap well in aluminum foil and store at room temperature.

# • PUMPKIN-MAPLE COFFEE CAKE •

*Makes 9 slices*

*Cake*
1 1/2 cups unbleached all-purpose
 flour
3/4 cup firmly packed light brown
 sugar
2 teaspoons baking
 powder
1/2 teaspoon salt
1/4 teaspoon baking soda
2/3 cup buttermilk

1/2 cup canned pumpkin (not
 pumpkin pie filling)
1/3 cup canola oil
1 tablespoon pure maple syrup
2 large eggs, beaten

*Topping*
1/2 cup granulated sugar
1 teaspoon ground cinnamon
1 teaspoon pure maple syrup

**1.** Preheat the oven to 350°F. Spray the bottom only of a 9-inch square pan with nonstick cooking spray.

**2.** Combine the flour and all the remaining cake ingredients in a medium bowl; mix just until the dry ingredients are moistened.

**3.** Make the topping: Stir together the sugar and cinnamon in a small bowl. Add the maple syrup; mix well with a fork.

**4.** Spread half of the batter evenly in the prepared pan. Sprinkle with half of the topping. Top with the remaining batter, using a rubber spatula to smooth. Sprinkle with the remaining topping.

**5.** Bake for 25 to 35 minutes, or until a toothpick inserted in the center comes out clean. Cool in the pan for 15 minutes before cutting into squares.

# · BLUEBERRY STREUSEL COFFEE CAKE ·

*Makes about 16 slices*

*Topping*

⅓ cup unbleached all-purpose flour

⅓ cup lightly packed light brown
  sugar

¼ cup (½ stick) unsalted butter,
  softened

1 teaspoon ground cinnamon

*Cake*

¾ cup granulated sugar

¼ cup (½ stick) unsalted butter,
  softened

1 large egg

1 teaspoon vanilla extract

¾ cup milk

1¾ cups unbleached all-purpose
  flour

1 tablespoon baking powder

½ teaspoon salt

1½ cups fresh or thawed and drained
  frozen blueberries

**1.** Preheat the oven to 375°F. Lightly grease a 9-inch square cake pan with baking spray.

**2.** Make the topping: Combine all the ingredients in a small bowl and mix until crumbly. Set aside.

**3.** Make the cake: Using an electric mixer on medium speed, cream the sugar, butter, egg, and vanilla until thoroughly blended. Add the milk and mix until blended.

**4.** Combine the flour, baking powder, and salt in a small bowl; mix well. Add the floured mixture to the creamed mixture all at once and stir until just moistened. Spread half of the batter in the prepared pan. Spoon the blueberries over the batter. Spread the remaining batter over the berries.

**5.** Sprinkle the topping evenly over the batter, pressing the topping into the batter lightly. Bake for 40 to 45 minutes, or until a toothpick inserted in the center comes out clean. Let cool in the pan for 20 minutes before cutting into squares.

# · TANGY LIME-POPPY SEED CAKE ·

*This cake is commonly made with lemons but we think limes give it a more interesting flavor. The tangy-sweet syrup adds a great finish.*

### Makes 12 to 14 slices

*Cake*
1 cup milk
4 tablespoons poppy seeds
3 large eggs, separated, at room
   temperature
1 teaspoon almond extract
1 cup (2 sticks) unsalted butter,
   softened
1¼ cups granulated sugar

1 tablespoon plus 2 teaspoons finely
   grated lime zest
2 cups unbleached all-purpose flour
1 tablespoon baking powder
½ teaspoon salt

*Lime Syrup*
¾ cup confectioners' sugar
6 tablespoons lime juice

**1.** Preheat the oven to 325°F. Lightly grease a 10-inch springform pan with baking spray.

**2.** Combine the milk and poppy seeds in a small saucepan over medium heat. Heat, stirring, until very hot, but not boiling. Remove the pan from the heat. Let stand until the mixture is room temperature.

**3.** Using an electric mixer on high speed, beat the egg whites and almond extract in a medium bowl until stiff peaks form. Set aside.

**4.** Using an electric mixer on high speed, cream the butter and granulated sugar in a large bowl. Add the egg yolks, lime zest, and milk mixture and mix on high speed until completely blended.

**5.** Combine the flour, baking powder, and salt in a small bowl and stir into the butter mixture until thoroughly blended. Using a rubber spatula, fold in the egg white mixture until no white streaks remain. Spread the batter evenly in the prepared pan, smoothing the top with a rubber spatula.

**6.** Bake for about 1 hour, or until a toothpick inserted in the center comes out clean. Let stand in the pan for 10 minutes before removing the side of the pan.

**7.** Meanwhile, make the lime syrup: Combine 2 tablespoons hot water and confectioners' sugar in a small bowl; stir until smooth. Stir in the lime juice. Drizzle over the hot cake, allowing the syrup to soak in. Cool. Wrap tightly in aluminum foil and store at room temperature.

# · EGGNOG POUND CAKE ·

*Makes 16 slices*

1³/₄ cups unbleached all-purpose
   flour
2 teaspoons baking powder
¹/₂ teaspoon salt
¹/₂ teaspoon ground nutmeg
¹/₂ teaspoon cinnamon
1 cup sugar

¹/₂ cup (1 stick) unsalted butter,
   softened
2 tablespoons dark rum
2 teaspoons vanilla extract
5 large egg yolks
³/₄ cup milk

**1.** Preheat the oven to 350°F. Grease and flour a 9×5×3-inch loaf pan. Combine the flour, baking powder, salt, and spices in a small bowl.

**2.** Using an electric mixer on low speed, beat the sugar, butter, rum, vanilla, and egg yolks in a large bowl for 60 seconds, scraping the bowl frequently. Increase the speed to high and beat for 5 minutes, scraping the bowl occasionally. Reduce the speed to low and mix in one-third of the flour mixture, alternating with the milk until just combined. Pour the batter into the prepared pan.

**3.** Bake for 50 to 60 minutes, or until a toothpick inserted in the center comes out clean. Cool in the pan for 10 minutes; remove from the pan and cool completely.

# · CHOCOLATE CHIP-POPPY SEED CAKE ·

*This cake seems to be equally popular at morning and evening bake sales.*

*Makes 12 to 16 slices*

2½ cups unbleached all-purpose flour
2 teaspoons baking powder
1 teaspoon baking soda
½ teaspoon salt
1 cup (2 sticks) unsalted butter, at room temperature
1 cup plus 4 tablespoons granulated sugar
2 teaspoons vanilla extract
1 teaspoon ground cinnamon

4 large eggs, separated, at room temperature
1 cup buttermilk, at room temperature
1 cup (6 ounces) mini semisweet chocolate chips
1½ ounces finely grated unsweetened chocolate
½ cup poppy seeds
Confectioners' sugar, for dusting

**1.** Position an oven rack in the center of the oven. Preheat the oven to 350°F. Grease a 12-cup Bundt pan. In a small bowl, sift the flour, baking powder, baking soda, and salt.

**2.** Using an electric mixer on medium speed, cream the butter, 1 cup plus 1 tablespoon of the sugar, the vanilla, and the cinnamon until blended, stopping the mixer once or twice to scrape the bowl with a rubber spatula. Add the egg yolks and beat on medium speed until blended, stopping to scrape the bowl once.

**3.** Using a rubber spatula, fold in one-third of the dry ingredients. Then fold in half of the the buttermilk, another third of the dry ingredients, the remaining buttermilk, and the remaining dry ingredients. Do not overmix; the ingredients will not be fully blended until the end of the mixing.

**4.** Using an electric mixer with clean beaters on medium-high speed, beat the egg whites in a clean medium bowl until foamy. With the mixer running, gradually add the remaining 3 tablespoons sugar and continue beating until soft peaks form. Using a wooden spoon, stir one-third of the whites into the batter, then fold in the rest of the whites with a rubber spatula. Fold in the chocolate chips, grated chocolate, and poppy seeds.

**5.** Scoop the batter into the pan and smooth the top with a rubber spatula. Bake the cake on the center oven rack until it is golden and a tester inserted in the center comes out dry, about 1 hour. Let the cake cool completely in the pan. Store, wrapped tightly in aluminum foil, at room temperature.

**6.** Just before bringing over to the bake sale, remove the cake from the pan and sift confectioners' sugar over it.

# · COCONUT-ORANGE CAKE ·

*Makes 16 servings*

2 cups unbleached all-purpose flour

1½ cups sugar

1 cup sweetened flaked coconut

½ cup unsalted butter, softened

1 cup milk

3½ teaspoons baking powder

1 tablespoon finely grated orange zest

½ teaspoon salt

2 teaspoons vanilla extract

3 eggs, lightly beaten

*Fluffy Orange Frosting*

½ cup sugar

¼ cup light corn syrup

2 large egg whites

2 teaspoons finely grated orange zest

**1.** Preheat the oven to 350°F. Grease and flour two 9½-inch round cake pans.

**2.** Using an electric mixer on medium speed, beat the flour, sugar, coconut, butter, milk, baking powder, zest, salt, vanilla, and eggs for 30 seconds, scraping the bowl constantly. Increase the speed to high and beat for 3 minutes, scraping the bowl occasionally. Pour the batter into the prepared pans.

**3.** Bake for 30 to 35 minutes, or until a toothpick inserted in the center comes out clean. Cool in the pans for 10 minutes; remove the layers and cool completely on a wire rack before frosting.

**4.** Meanwhile, make the fluffy orange frosting: Stir together the sugar, corn syrup, and 2 tablespoons water in a 1-quart covered saucepan over medium heat. Cover and heat to a rolling boil. Uncover and boil rapidly until the mixture reaches 242°F on a candy thermometer (soft-ball stage; a small amount of mixture dropped into very cold water forms a ball that flattens when removed from the water).

**5.** Meanwhile, using an electric mixer on high speed, beat the egg whites in a medium bowl just until stiff peaks form. Reduce the speed to medium, and with the mixer running, carefully pour the hot syrup very slowly in a thin stream into the egg whites. Increase the speed to high and beat until stiff. Fold in the orange zest.

**6.** Frost the top of one layer and stack the other layer on top. Frost the sides, then the top of the cake.

**7.** Store this cake at room temperature in a cake saver.

"I've never been a big fan of coconut and lemon together, so I was thrilled to find this recipe using orange as the citrus. I love the orange frosting, which is also great on plain vanilla cupcakes."

—Dahlia A., New Rochelle, New York

Some people shop a bake sale looking for something whole to bring home. Here are a favorite cake and a favorite pie, both of which benefit from being sold whole.

### TURTLE CAKE · Makes 1 cake

Spectacularly rich, this cake is special enough to be auctioned off. In fact, when Laurie did just that recently she raised $60 for her bake sale!

**Caramel-Pecan Filling**

*1 cup (2 sticks) unsalted butter*

*2 cups granulated sugar*

*2 tablespoons light corn syrup*

*1 cup heavy cream*

*1 cup chopped pecans, toasted and cooled*


**Cake**

*2 cups unbleached all-purpose flour*

*1 teaspoon baking soda*

*½ teaspoon salt*

*1½ cups (18 ounces) semisweet chocolate chips*

*½ cup (1 stick) unsalted butter, softened*

*One 16-ounce box light brown sugar*

*3 large eggs*

*1 cup sour cream*

*1 tablespoon vanilla extract*


**Chocolate Ganache**

*1 package (12 ounces) semisweet chocolate chips*

*½ cup heavy cream*

*3 tablespoons unsalted butter*

1. Make the caramel-pecan filling: Melt the butter in a heavy 3-quart saucepan over medium heat. Add the sugar and the corn syrup and cook, stirring constantly, until the syrup becomes a deep caramel color, 6 to 8 minutes.

2. Add the heavy cream and cook, stirring constantly, for 1 to 2 minutes. (The mixture will bubble up.)

3. Remove the pan from the heat and let cool to room temperature. Place in the refrigerator and chill until the sauce has thickened to spreading consistency, at least 3 hours and up to overnight.

4. Make the cake: Preheat the oven to 350°F. Spray three 9-inch round cake pans with baking spray. Sift together the flour, baking soda, and salt into a large bowl.

5. Microwave the chocolate chips on medium (50%) power, stirring at 30-second intervals, just until melted, 2 to 3 minutes. Stir until smooth.

6. Using an electric mixer on medium speed, beat the butter and brown sugar until well blended. Add the eggs, one at a time, beating on medium speed after each addition. Stir in the melted chocolate.

7. Gradually add the dry ingredients, alternating with the sour cream, starting and ending with the dry. Stir until thoroughly blended. Do not overbeat.

8. Add 1 cup hot water in a slow stream, stirring constantly until blended. Stir in the vanilla.

9. Pour the batter into the pans. Bake for 25 to 30 minutes until a cake tester or toothpick comes out clean. Cool thoroughly in the pans on a wire rack.

10. Just before assembling, make the chocolate ganache: Heat the chocolate chips and the heavy cream on medium (50%) power, stirring at 30-second intervals, until the chocolate starts to melt, 2 to 3 minutes. Whisk until the mixture is smooth. Whisk in the butter and let stand for 30 minutes.

11. Using an electric mixer on medium speed, beat until the mixture forms soft peaks, 3 to 4 minutes.

12. Assemble the cake: Place one cake layer on a serving platter. With a spatula or the back of a large spoon, spread 1 cup of the caramel sauce over the top in an even layer and sprinkle with ⅓ cup chopped pecans. Repeat with the remaining cake layers, caramel sauce, and pecans, ending with a caramel-pecan layer.

13. With an offset spatula, spread the chocolate ganache in an even layer around the sides of the cake. Let stand until the ganache has set, 30 minutes.

## APPLE-PRALINE PIE · Makes 1 pie

Use a 9- or 10-inch aluminum tin to bake this extra-special apple pie in. We like to use Granny Smith apples, but any tart variety will work. It's a beauty!

*2 recipes Single-Crust Pie Pastry (page 137) or 2 refrigerated piecrusts*
*1 cup granulated sugar*
*⅔ cup chopped pecans*
*⅓ cup unbleached all-purpose flour*
*1 teaspoon ground cinnamon*
*1 teaspoon ground nutmeg*
*¼ teaspoon salt*
*8 cups peeled and thinly sliced tart apples (about 7 medium apples)*
*3 tablespoons unsalted butter or margarine, cut into cubes*
*¼ cup packed light brown sugar*
*2 tablespoons half-and-half*
*¾ cup pecan halves, for topping*

1. Preheat the oven to 425°F.

2. Prepare the piecrust. Using a floured rolling pin, roll out one disk of dough until it is 2 inches larger than an inverted pie plate placed over it.

3. Carefully fold the pastry into fourths; unfold and ease into the pie plate, pressing firmly against the bottom and side. Chill for 15 minutes.

4. In a large bowl, mix together the granulated sugar, pecans, flour, cinnamon, nutmeg, and salt. Add the apples and toss until coated.

5. Turn the apple mixture into the pastry-lined pie plate. Dot with butter. On a lightly floured surface, roll out the top crust to at least 11 inches in diameter. Carefully wrap the crust around the rolling pin and gently lay it over the top of the filled pie. Crimp the two edges together to seal. Make three slits in the top crust so heat can escape. Cover the edge with a 2- to 3-inch strip of aluminum foil to prevent excessive browning; remove the foil during the last 15 minutes of baking.

6. Bake for 50 to 60 minutes, until the crust is brown and juice begins to bubble through the slits in the crust.

7. Mix the brown sugar and the half-and-half in a 1-quart saucepan. Cook over low heat, stirring constantly, until the sugar is melted. Spread over the hot pie; top with pecan halves.

**TIP:** Sell this pie in the tin, wrapped in cellophane from the bottom up.

# Seven

## Cupcakes Galore

*These days cupcakes are everywhere—so they'd better be at your bake sale, too. From Ladybugs for tiny ones to Coconut Mountains for the sophisticated palates, you can't go wrong with unique cupcakes at a bake sale.*

*When it comes to transporting cupcakes, our secret weapon is a cupcake carrier (see Resources, page 247), which gets dozens of cupcakes from kitchen to bake sale with decorations intact. We like to display them on flat, round platters or on poster board covered with aluminum foil.*

# • BEST VANILLA CUPCAKES •

*These cupcakes are light and have a super vanilla-y taste. They're perfect for any of our recipes that start with white cupcakes.*

*Makes 24 cupcakes*

2 cups unbleached all-purpose flour, sifted
2 teaspoons baking powder
½ teaspoon salt

½ cup (1 stick) unsalted butter, softened
1 cup sugar
2 eggs
2 teaspoons vanilla extract

**1.** Heat the oven to 375°F. Line two 12-cup cupcake pans with paper liners.

**2.** In a large mixing bowl, combine the flour, baking powder, and salt. Set aside.

**3.** In another large bowl, beat the butter and sugar until light and fluffy. Add the eggs, one at a time, beating well after each addition. Add the vanilla.

**4.** Slowly add the wet mixture to the dry ingredients and stir with a wooden spoon until well combined.

**5.** Divide the batter among the paper liners. Bake for 20 to 23 minutes until the cupcakes are light golden brown. Cool in the pans for 10 minutes, then transfer to a wire rack to cool completely before decorating.

# · BEST CHOCOLATE CUPCAKES ·

*Moist and not too sweet, these cupcakes work equally well with a rich frosting or just a sprinkling of powdered sugar. This is a fantastic basic recipe when you want to make a special treat that starts with a chocolate cupcake.*

## *Makes 24 cupcakes*

4 ounces (4 squares) unsweetened chocolate

2 cups sugar

2 cups unbleached all-purpose flour

$^3/_4$ teaspoon baking soda

$^1/_2$ teaspoon salt

$^1/_2$ cup hot strong coffee

$^1/_2$ cup sour cream, at room temperature

$^1/_2$ cup canola oil

2 large eggs, lightly beaten

**1.** Preheat the oven to 350°F. Line two 12-cup cupcake pans with paper liners. On top of a double boiler, heat the chocolate until fully melted. Combine the sugar, flour, baking soda, and salt in a large mixing bowl. Set aside.

**2.** Using an electric mixer on medium speed, beat the hot coffee, sour cream, and canola oil until well blended, about 2 minutes.

**3.** Slowly add the coffee mixture to the dry ingredients and stir well. Add the eggs and beat on low speed until just combined. Add the melted chocolate and mix until blended.

**4.** Divide the batter evenly among the paper liners. Bake for 25 to 30 minutes, or until the cupcakes spring back to the touch when pressed gently in the center. Cool in the pans for 10 minutes, then transfer to a wire rack to cool completely before decorating.

# · CHOCOLATE CUPCAKES THAT START WITH A MIX ·

*We're fans of cake mixes, especially when it comes to school bake sales. Here, we give the boxed mix a little boost, making these extra-chocolaty.*

*Makes 24 cupcakes*

| | |
|---|---|
| One 18.25-ounce package devil's food cake mix | ½ cup canola oil |
| 3 large eggs | 1 cup (6 ounces) mini chocolate chips |

**1.** Preheat the oven to 350°F. Line two 12-cup cupcake pans with paper liners.

**2.** Combine all the ingredients and 1⅓ cups water in a large bowl. Using an electric mixer on low speed, beat for 4 minutes, stopping halfway through to scrape down the sides of the bowl.

**3.** Divide the batter evenly among the paper liners. Bake for 25 to 30 minutes, or until the cupcakes spring back to the touch when pressed gently in the center. Cool in the pans for 10 minutes, then transfer to a wire rack to cool completely before decorating.

**TIP**

There are many kinds of mixes to choose from these days, including peanut-free, dairy-free, wheat- and gluten-free varieties. Two terrific brands are Bob's Red Mill and Cherrybrook Kitchen. Food-sensitive patrons are hugely grateful to see something they can eat at a bake sale.

# • VANILLA CUPCAKES THAT START WITH A MIX •

*French vanilla cake mix is the flavor we used, though any vanilla cake mix will work for a basic cupcake that is ready to decorate, which is what cupcakes are all about at bake sales.*

### Makes 24 cupcakes

One 18.25-ounce package vanilla cake mix

3 large eggs

½ cup (1 stick) unsalted butter, softened

**1.** Preheat the oven to 350°F. Line two 12-cup cupcake pans with paper liners.

**2.** Combine all the ingredients and 1¼ cups water in a large bowl. Using an electric mixer on low speed, beat for 4 minutes, stopping halfway through to scrape down the sides of the bowl.

**3.** Divide the batter evenly among the paper liners. Bake for 25 to 30 minutes, or until the cupcakes spring back to the touch when pressed gently in the center. Cool in the pans for 10 minutes, then transfer to a wire rack to cool completely before decorating.

# • SUPER-EASY CHOCOLATE-CREAM CHEESE FROSTING •

*Makes 4 cups (enough for 3 to 4 dozen cupcakes)*

One 8-ounce package cream cheese, softened

½ cup (1 stick) unsweetened butter, softened

½ cup unsweetened cocoa powder

2 teaspoons vanilla extract

4 cups confectioners' sugar, sifted

**1.** Combine the cream cheese and butter in a large bowl. Using an electric mixer on low speed, beat for 1 minute to mix.

**2.** Add the remaining ingredients and beat on medium speed for 3 minutes, or until fluffy.

# · VANILLA BUTTERCREAM FROSTING ·

*Makes 3¾ cups (enough for 3 to 4 dozen cupcakes)*

½ cup (1 stick) unsalted butter,
   softened
3¾ cups confectioners' sugar

3 to 4 tablespoons half-and-half
2 teaspoons vanilla extract

**1.** Combine the butter and sugar in a large bowl. Stir together the half-and-half and vanilla in a small bowl or glass measuring cup.

**2.** Using an electric mixer on medium speed, beat the butter and sugar until creamy. Turn the mixer to low speed and gradually add the half-and-half and vanilla, scraping the bowl often, until well mixed. Beat until light and fluffy.

# · CHOCOLATE BUTTERCREAM FROSTING ·

*Makes about 5 cups (enough for 3 to 4 dozen cupcakes)*

5 cups confectioners' sugar
$^{1}/_{2}$ cup unsweetened cocoa powder
Dash of salt
2 ounces (2 squares) unsweetened
   baking chocolate, melted

$^{1}/_{2}$ cup heavy cream
1 cup (2 sticks) unsalted butter,
   softened

**1.** Combine the confectioners' sugar, cocoa, and salt in a medium bowl. Stir together the melted chocolate and heavy cream in a small bowl or glass measuring cup.

**2.** Using an electric mixer on medium speed, beat the butter in a large bowl until creamy. Turn the mixer to low speed and gradually add the confectioners' sugar mixture alternately with the cream mixture, scraping the bowl often, until well mixed.

# · SEVEN-MINUTE FROSTING ·

*This dairy-free frosting is pure white and purely delicious. It can be tinted with food coloring into lovely pastel shades.*

*Makes 4 cups (enough for 24 cupcakes)*

| | |
|---|---|
| 1½ cups sugar | ¼ teaspoon cream of tartar |
| 2 egg whites | 1 teaspoon vanilla extract |

**1.** Heat 2 inches of water in a medium saucepan or the bottom of a double boiler over medium-high heat until boiling. Combine all the ingredients except the vanilla with ⅓ cup water in a medium heatproof bowl. Using an electric mixer on high speed, beat until combined.

**2.** Set the bowl over the boiling water (the bottom should not touch the water) and continue beating on high until it holds stiff, glossy peaks, about 7 minutes. (Depending on the mixer and the weather this may take longer than 7 minutes.)

**3.** Remove the bowl from the heat and beat in the vanilla. Beat the frosting on high speed until cooled and spreadable, 3 to 5 minutes.

# · PEACE SIGN CUPCAKES ·

*This decoration works best if the cupcakes are not too rounded on the top. Before baking, use a teaspoon to push the batter from the center toward the edges of the cups so the batter is slightly concave. Alternatively, just cut off the top with a sharp serrated knife after they're baked.*

*Makes 24 cupcakes*

1 recipe Vanilla Buttercream Frosting (page 171)
24 chocolate or vanilla cupcakes (pages 167 and 166), baked and cooled

Lots of dragées or other small, round candies, such as Red Hots

**1.** Using a small offset spatula, frost the cupcakes, keeping the frosting as flat as possible. Refrigerate the frosted cupcakes for 1 hour.

**2.** Using a toothpick, carefully draw the outline of a peace sign on the top of each cupcake. Cover the outline with single dragées or small candies.

> **TIP**
>
> Clean, long-handled tweezers are helpful in placing the candies. A toothpick will work, too.

" My son Henry and I have made these peace sign cupcakes for bake sales. Not only do they go fast, but the message makes people stop and talk. It's a nice way to meet like-minded people in our community. "

—Emily W., Brooklyn, New York

# · FLOWER POWER ·

*Makes 24 cupcakes*

1 recipe Vanilla Buttercream
 Frosting (page 171)
24 vanilla cupcakes (page 166), baked
 and cooled

24 M&M's or gumdrops
About 100 marshmallows

**1.** Frost the cupcakes. Place a candy in the center of each cupcake.

**2.** Cut the marshmallows in half crosswise. Pull the marshmallow halves and pinch the ends to make into oval (petal) shapes.

**3.** Arrange 5 marshmallow pieces around the candy in a flower shape.

**TIP**

Decorate the cupcakes in a variety of colors, with different candy centers on each one. Make a "flower arrangement" on a large platter—it will be the hit of the bake sale table.

# · WITCHES' "HAT" CHOCOLATE ·

*These witches' hats are fun for kids to help with, placing the cone
on the cupcake and adding the sprinkles, too. Terrific for Halloween, but
they'll sell anytime, especially to young buyers.*

### Makes 24 cupcakes

1 recipe Chocolate Buttercream
Frosting (page 172) or one
1-pound can prepared chocolate
frosting

24 chocolate cupcakes (page 167),
baked and cooled

24 chocolate-coated sugar ice cream
cones

Purple or orange sprinkles

Frost the cupcakes with a thick layer of frosting. Place the cones upside down, pressing into the frosting. Decorate the edges of the cupcakes with the sprinkles.

# · COCONUT MOUNTAINS ·

*This simple decorating idea looks beautiful on both cupcakes and whole cakes. You can use shredded coconut, but we prefer to use unsweetened coconut chips. Arrange the cupcakes on a tiered platter for a dramatic mountain effect.*

*Makes 24 cupcakes*

1 recipe Seven-Minute Frosting (page 173) or one 1-pound can white chocolate frosting

24 vanilla cupcakes (page 166), baked in white paper liners and cooled

2 to 3 cups unsweetened coconut chips (see Tip)

Frost the cupcakes with white frosting. Cover each cupcake with coconut chips, pressing them in gently. (It's best to do this while the frosting is still soft.)

**TIP**

Coconut chips look like shavings. You can buy them online from www.nutsonline.com, or at a baking supply store (see Resources, page 247).

# · TIC TAC TOE ·

*These colorful cupcakes will fly off the table if kids are buying! We like
the way they look with brightly colored frosting in, say, yellow, pink, or green.
This decoration works best if the cupcakes are not too rounded on the top;
see Peace Sign Cupcakes, page 174, for tips.*

## Makes 24 cupcakes

One 1-pound can white chocolate
frosting, brightly tinted with
food coloring
24 chocolate or vanilla cupcakes
(pages 167 and 166), baked and
cooled

96 pretzel sticks
One 12-ounce package M&M's
chocolate mini baking bits

**1.** Using a small offset spatula, frost the cupcakes, keeping the frosting as flat as
possible.

**2.** Lay two pretzel sticks parallel to each other on the top of each cupcake. Break two
pretzels into three pieces each and place them perpendicular to the whole sticks to
make a tic-tac-toe board. Fill in the squares with the mini M&M's shaped into Xs
and Os in contrasting colors.

**TIP**

We've found that canned white chocolate frosting (Betty Crocker and Duncan
Hines both make it), which is pure white, is just right for these cupcakes.

# · PINK PARASOLS ·

*These paper parasols are real attention-getters, especially when you set up a whole tray of them. The multitude of open umbrellas is beautiful!*

## Makes 24 cupcakes

1 recipe Seven-Minute Frosting (page 173), tinted pale pink, or one 1-pound can storebought strawberry frosting

24 vanilla cupcakes (page 166), baked and cooled

One 12-ounce package M&M's chocolate mini baking bits

24 mini paper cocktail parasols

**1.** Frost the cupcakes with the pale pink frosting. While the frosting is still wet, sprinkle the baking bits over the tops of the cupcakes.

**2.** Place an open paper parasol into the top of each cupcake, tilting it slightly off center. Let stand until the frosting is set, about 30 minutes.

> **TIP**
>
> Cocktail parasols are available at many party stores or online from House of Rice Store (www.houserice.com). They cost about $2 for a package of 24.

# · ELECTRIC CUPCAKES ·

*People will see these from across the room! We like to use contrasting colors of frosting and sprinkles, such as green with pink and yellow with blue.*

## Makes 24 cupcakes

3 to 4 cups Vanilla Buttercream
Frosting (page 171) or one
1-pound can vanilla frosting
Assorted neon food coloring

24 vanilla cupcakes (page 166),
baked and cooled
Sprinkles in neon colors

**1.** Divide the frosting among small bowls; use one bowl for each color you want to make. Color with neon-colored food coloring.

**2.** Frost the cupcakes generously in one color, then top with sprinkles in a contrasting color.

**TIP**
Neon-colored sprinkles and food coloring are available from www.wilton.com or baking-supply stores.

# · LADYBUGS ·

*Kids generally like insects, and ladybugs rate right up there on their list of favorites. These are ideal for a preschool bake sale.*

## Makes 24 cupcakes

1 recipe Vanilla Buttercream Frosting (page 171) or one 1-pound can white chocolate frosting, tinted red
24 vanilla cupcakes (page 166), baked in red paper liners and cooled

Black licorice laces, cut into 24 three-inch lengths and 48 one-inch lengths
One 12-ounce package mini chocolate chips

**1.** Frost the cupcakes, making the frosting rounded and smooth. Refrigerate for at least 1 hour and up to overnight.

**2.** Using a toothpick or a wooden skewer, make a line running down the center of the cupcake, then gently press a 3-inch length of licorice into the line. Push two 1-inch pieces into the edge of the cupcake, one on either side of the line, for antennae. Push the chocolate chips point side down into the frosting to make the ladybug's spots. Repeat with remaining cupcakes, licorice, and chocolate chips.

**TIP** www. sugarcraft.com has a wide variety of colored cupcake liners if you can't find red ones locally.

# · GRIBBIT CUPCAKES ·

*Cute frogs, anyone? The jelly-ring eyes on these critters are very hard to pass up.*

## Makes 24 cupcakes

1 recipe Vanilla Buttercream
   Frosting (page 171) or one 1-pound
   can vanilla frosting, tinted green
24 vanilla cupcakes (page 166),
   baked in green paper liners and
   cooled completely

48 green jelly rings
48 chocolate chips
Several lengths of black or red string
   licorice, cut into 1-inch lengths

Frost the cupcakes with bright green frosting. Place two jelly rings so that part of each ring goes over the edge of the cupcake, like a frog's eyes. Center a chocolate chip in each ring and press it point side down into the frosting. Gently press the licorice in place for the mouth.

# · SNAKES ON A PLATE ·

*There are lots of candy snakes available these days.*
*Choose the ones you find least terrifying.*

*Makes 24 cupcakes*

1 recipe Vanilla Buttercream
  Frosting (page 171) or one 1-pound
  can white chocolate frosting,
  tinted any shade you desire

24 chocolate or vanilla cupcakes
  (pages 167 and 166), baked and
  cooled
72 gummy snakes

Frost the cupcakes, piling the frosting on high. You'll need three snakes for each cupcake. Push the ends of the snakes down into the frosting (use a toothpick or wooden skewer if you need to), letting them hang down the cupcakes in different directions. (You may need to smooth out the frosting where the snakes come out of it.)

# · EDIBLE FLOWER CUPCAKES ·

*A cupcake decorated with a real, edible flower is a lovely-looking treat. Whole Foods markets often carry little containers of pretty (and good to eat) flora in the produce section, near the herbs. Icing flowers are another way to go.*

### Makes 24 cupcakes

3 cups frosting, any colors

24 cupcakes, any flavor, baked and
  cooled

24 to 40 edible flowers

**1.** Divide the frosting among bowls, one for each color. Tint to desired shade.

**2.** Frost the cupcakes using a small spatula or spreader.

**3.** Top the frosted cupcakes with one or two flowers or flower petals.

> "It's nice to make cupcakes that adults appreciate for a change. These are sophisticated and delicious. I made them for our temple's bake sale and they were a big hit."
>
> —Josh A., Brookline, Massachusetts

# · THIS LITTLE PIGGY ·

*Pigs never looked so cute. (Well, maybe Babe, but that's it.) If you need a color reference for the frosting, check out Crayola's 64-crayon box for the color "Piggy Pink."*

### *Makes 24 cupcakes*

1 recipe Seven-Minute Frosting (page 173) or one 1-pound can white chocolate frosting, tinted pink

24 vanilla cupcakes (page 166), baked in pink liners and cooled

72 marshmallows, cut in half crosswise

1 small tube white decorating frosting

Mini chocolate morsels

**1.** Frost the cupcakes with pink frosting. Place a marshmallow half in the center of each cupcake, cut side down. Make two dots of frosting on the marshmallow and press two chocolate chips into the dots of frosting for nostrils.

**2.** Squeeze two marshmallow halves on one end to make ears and press into the frosting at the top of the cupcake (where the ears would be). Use chocolate morsels for the eyes. Oink!

# • CHOCOLATE TEDDY BEARS •

*These cupcakes are so moist and delicious, no one will guess they're made with a mix. They stay moist for up to 3 days, so you can bake them ahead.*

## Makes 24 cupcakes

One 18.25-ounce package dark
　　chocolate cake mix
One 3.4-ounce package instant
　　chocolate pudding
4 large eggs
1 cup sour cream
½ cup canola oil

2 teaspoons vanilla extract
1 cup milk chocolate morsels
1 recipe Super-Easy Chocolate–
　　Cream Cheese Frosting (page 170)
48 small candy eyes or Red Hots
24 red or pink jellybeans
48 mini chocolate sandwich cookies

**1.** Preheat the oven to 350°F. Line two 12-cup muffin tins with paper liners and set aside.

**2.** Combine the cake mix, pudding mix, eggs, sour cream, ½ cup warm water, oil, and vanilla in a large bowl. Using an electric mixer on medium speed, beat for 2 to 3 minutes, stopping halfway to scrape down the sides of the bowl, until thick and well combined. Fold in the chocolate morsels.

**3.** Divide the batter evenly among the paper liners. Bake the cupcakes for 20 to 25 minutes, or until the top of a cake springs back when lightly pressed in the center. Cool in the pan for 20 minutes, then transfer to a wire rack to cool completely before decorating.

**4.** To decorate, spread each cupcake with about 2 tablespoons frosting. Use a small spatula and make the frosting as smooth and flat as possible.

**5.** Place two candy eyes or red hots on the top half of each cupcake. Place a jellybean below the eyes (vertically) for the nose and mouth.

**6.** With a small sharp knife cut off one-third of each mini cookie, discarding the smaller pieces (or save them for snacking). Press a cookie into the frosting above each eye for ears.

> "We sold these at our elementary school's winter carnival for $2 apiece—I thought that was high until they were the first item we were sold out of!"

—Beth R., North Haven, Connecticut

# • TEEPEE CUPCAKES •

*Two cupcakes form the base of these ingenious treats, which get a thin layer of fondant as the tent covering.*

## Makes 24 cupcakes

24 regular-size cupcakes, any flavor, baked and cooled

24 store-bought mini cupcakes, any flavor

1 recipe Vanilla or Chocolate Buttercream Frosting (pages 171 and 172)

72 pretzel sticks

Brown food coloring gel

2 pounds white fondant, at room temperature

Small tubes of decorating gel in red and black

**1.** Place a regular-size cupcake on your work surface. Frost and top it with a mini cupcake. Push three pretzel sticks in the frosting on the regular cupcake so that the tops cross in the center of the mini cupcake (like the sticks that poke out of the top of a teepee). Repeat with the remaining frosting, cupcakes, and pretzels.

**2.** Use a toothpick to scoop out a small blob of food coloring to add to the fondant. Knead the fondant until the color is blended. Break the fondant into lemon-size ovals and roll each one out to a rounded rectangle. Ultimately you'll want a rectangle for each teepee, but roll and drape one or two at a time as the rolled fondant can dry out.

**3.** Drape a piece of fondant around each cupcake, folding to form a curtain effect in the front. Decorate the sides of the teepee with symbols in different gel colors.

**NOTE:** Once draped, these cupcakes can be stored at room temperature for up to 2 days.

> **TIP**
>
> Transport these cupcakes to the bake sale in a box covered with aluminum foil.

# · ONE-EYED CUPCAKES ·

*These go over well at bake sales, where elementary-school kids appreciate the gross factor.*

*Makes 24 cupcakes*

3 cups Seven-Minute Frosting (page 173)

24 vanilla cupcakes (page 166), baked and cooled

24 round red candies, such as gumballs, sour balls, or firecrackers

1 tube red decorating gel

Frost the cupcakes. Place a red candy in the center of the frosting. Using the red gel, make squiggly lines from the eyeball out to look like blood vessels.

# · GONE FISHING ·

*This cupcake is Laurie's daughter Olivia's favorite.*

## Makes 24 cupcakes

1 recipe Vanilla Buttercream
Frosting (page 171)
Blue food coloring
24 vanilla cupcakes (page 166),
baked and cooled

24 red Swedish fish candies
About 60 to 70 dragées

**1.** Tint the frosting to the desired shade with the blue food coloring.

**2.** Frost the cupcakes, then run the tines of a fork through the frosting to look like waves.

**3.** Place a Swedish fish in the center of the frosting, then add a few dragées going up from the fish's mouth for bubbles.

# · UP, UP, AND AWAY ·

*A bouquet of balloon cupcakes makes a beautiful display at a bake sale.*
*Use a nice variety of colors to frost the balloons.*

## Makes 24 cupcakes

2 cups Vanilla Buttercream Frosting
(page 171)
Food coloring, in assorted colors

24 vanilla cupcakes (page 166),
baked in liners of various colors
and cooled
Colorful string (about 8 yards)

**1.** Divide the frosting among bowls, using a different bowl for each color. Frost the cupcakes.

**2.** Tape the string in varying lengths to a serving platter and tie the ends of the string to resemble the string on a bunch of balloons. (Make sure the strings are long enough to drape over the edge of your bake sale table.)

**3.** Arrange the cupcakes on the serving platter to resemble a bunch of balloons. The strings can hang off the table.

# · PRICKLY PORCUPINES ·

*Simple and yummy.*

---

*Makes 24 cupcakes*

24 chocolate cupcakes (page 167), baked and cooled

3 cups Super-Easy Chocolate–Cream Cheese Frosting (page 170)

3 cups slivered almonds

48 chocolate chips

**1.** Frost the cupcakes with the chocolate frosting.

**2.** Cover each cupcake with slivered almond "quills." Place two chocolate chips for eyes.

# · MINTALICIOUS CUPCAKES ·

*Makes 24 cupcakes*

½ teaspoon peppermint extract
1 recipe vanilla or chocolate
cupcakes (pages 166 and 167),
unbaked

50 peppermint candies
3 cups Seven-Minute Frosting (page
173), tinted pale pink, if desired

**1.** Stir the peppermint extract into the cupcake batter, fill 24 baking cups, and bake as directed. Let cool completely.

**2.** Meanwhile, pour the peppermint candies into a resealable plastic bag. Use a rolling pin or heavy pan to crush them. Pour the crushed candy into a shallow bowl.

**3.** Frost the cupcakes with pink or white frosting. Lightly press each cupcake into the crushed candy, gently tapping it on the side of the bowl to shake off excess candy.

# · NORTH POLE ·

*We first saw these at a winter carnival bake sale. They are frosted white,*
*with shredded coconut and a mini candy cane and little animal-cracker*
*reindeer perched on top.*

## *Makes 24 cupcakes*

3 cups Seven-Minute Frosting
   (page 173)
24 vanilla cupcakes (page 166), baked
   and cooled

2 cups shredded coconut
24 mini candy canes
24 animal crackers or small
   plastic reindeer

Frost the cupcakes with the white frosting. Sprinkle with the shredded coconut.
Push a candy cane into each cupcake; set an animal cracker or a plastic reindeer
next to it.

**NOTE:** Small toys pose a choking hazard for children under four.

**TIP** Plastic toys can be purchased in bulk from dollar stores. Before using, soak
them in a bowl of hot, sudsy water. Rinse thoroughly and let dry on paper towels.

# Eight

## Not from Scratch

*Slice-and-bake cookies or brownies from a mix are a considerably better contribution to a bake sale than a box of the store-bought kind or, worse, nothing at all. So next time you want to contribute to a bake sale but are short on time, try one of these recipes. Also, check out the twenty-four cupcakes in Chapter 7—all of which can start with a mix.*

# • PEANUT BUTTER CUP COOKIES •

*Part cookie, part candy, unbelievably simple.*

## Makes 36 cookies

One 20-ounce package refrigerated sugar cookie dough

36 miniature peanut butter cups, unwrapped

**1.** Preheat the oven to 350°F. Spray a miniature muffin pan with baking spray.

**2.** Divide the dough into 36 walnut-size balls, about 1 full tablespoon each. Press the dough lightly into the prepared muffin cups, pressing it up the sides. Bake for 10 to 12 minutes until golden brown.

**3.** Press a peanut butter cup into the center of each cookie cup. Cool completely in the pan.

# · BIRDS' NESTS ·

*These nests are very cute and can be filled with baking bits or other small candies. They're simple and delicious.*

*Makes 24 cookies*

One 20-ounce package refrigerated sugar cookie dough

1 cup toasted coconut (see Tip)

One 6-ounce package M&M's chocolate mini baking bits

**1.** Preheat the oven to 375°F. Grease two baking sheets with baking spray.

**2.** Form the cookie dough into 1¼-inch balls. Roll the dough in the toasted coconut.

**3.** Arrange the dough balls 2 inches apart on the prepared baking sheets. Using your thumb or the tip of a teaspoon, make an indentation in each cookie. Bake for 12 to 14 minutes, or until golden brown.

**4.** Allow to cool completely on the baking sheets. Fill the indentations with the mini baking bits.

> **TIP**
>
> Toasting coconut is a snap. Preheat the oven to 325°F. Spread the coconut in a single layer on a baking pan with sides. Bake, stirring frequently, until light golden brown, 5 to 7 minutes.

# • THUMBPRINTS •

*These cookies are absolutely delicious when made with Tiptree Little Scarlet Preserves, available in supermarkets.*

*Makes 26 cookies*

| One 20-ounce package refrigerated sugar or peanut butter cookie dough | $^{3}/_{4}$ cup plus 1 tablespoon fruit preserves, any flavor |
|---|---|

**1.** Preheat the oven to 350°F. Grease two baking sheets. Unwrap the tube of dough and lightly sprinkle the dough and the cutting board with flour.

**2.** Cut the dough into twenty-six 1-inch slices. With floured hands, roll the slices into balls. Arrange the dough balls 2 inches apart on the prepared baking sheets. Refrigerate for 20 minutes.

**3.** Bake the cookies for 10 to 12 minutes, or until the edges are golden brown (the cookies will have started to puff up in the center). Use the tip of a teaspoon to press an indentation into each cookie.

**4.** Return to the oven for 2 to 3 minutes, or until the cookies are golden brown and set. Cool completely on the baking sheets on a wire rack. Fill each cookie with about $1^{1}/_{2}$ teaspoons preserves.

**TIP**

For a change of pace, try filling these with Nutella, a chocolate-hazelnut spread available in most supermarkets.

# · PECAN BROWNIES ·

*Makes about 16 brownies*

| Brownies | Topping |
|---|---|
| One 1-pound, 3.5-ounce package milk chocolate brownie mix | $^3/_4$ cup firmly packed light brown sugar |
| 2 large eggs | $^3/_4$ cup chopped pecans |
| $^1/_3$ cup canola oil | $^1/_4$ cup ($^1/_2$ stick) unsalted butter, melted |
| $^2/_3$ cup chopped pecans | 2 tablespoons milk |
| | 1 teaspoon vanilla extract |

**1.** Preheat the oven to 350°F. Grease the bottom only of a 9-inch square pan.

**2.** Combine all the brownie ingredients and $^1/_3$ cup water in a large bowl. Using a wooden spoon, stir until well blended, about 50 strokes. Spread the batter in the prepared pan. Bake for 35 to 40 minutes, or until a cake tester comes out clean.

**3.** Meanwhile, make the topping: Stir the ingredients together in a small bowl until well blended. Spread over the hot brownies. Return the pan to the oven and bake for 15 minutes, or until the topping is set. Cool completely in the pan on a wire rack, then cut into squares.

# · DOUBLE "TOPPED" BROWNIES ·

*Mixes with a fudge packet are extra chewy and chocolaty. Make these when you want a superrich brownie.*

*Makes about 48 brownies*

**Brownies**
One 1-pound, 3.5-ounce package
   double-fudge brownie
   mix
2 large eggs
¼ cup vegetable oil
½ cup sweetened flaked coconut
⅓ cup chopped walnuts

**Frosting**
3 cups confectioners' sugar
5 tablespoons unsalted butter, softened
2 teaspoons vanilla extract
2 to 3 tablespoons milk

**Topping**
3 ounces (3 squares) semisweet
   chocolate
1 tablespoon unsalted butter

**1.** Preheat the oven to 350°F. Grease the bottom only of a 9×13-inch pan.

**2.** Stir together the brownie mix (including the fudge packet), eggs, oil, and ⅓ cup water in a large bowl until well blended, about 50 strokes. Stir in the coconut and nuts. Spread in the prepared pan. Bake for 27 to 30 minutes, or until set. Cool completely in the pan on a wire rack before frosting.

**3.** Make the frosting: Combine the confectioners' sugar, butter, and vanilla in a small bowl. Stir in the milk, 1 tablespoon at a time, until the frosting is of spreading consistency. Spread over the brownies in the pan. Refrigerate until the frosting is firm, about 30 minutes.

**4.** Meanwhile, make the topping: Melt the chocolate and butter in a small bowl over hot water; stir until smooth. Drizzle over the frosting. Refrigerate until the chocolate is firm, about 15 minutes, then cut into squares.

# · CHOCOLATE CHIP RASPBERRY JUMBLES ·

*Makes 16 bars*

1 17.5-ounce package chocolate chip
cookie mix

½ cup seedless red raspberry jam

**1.** Preheat the oven to 350°F.

**2.** Prepare the chocolate chip cookie mix as directed on the package.

**3.** Reserve ½ cup of the dough and spread the remaining dough into an ungreased 9-inch square baking pan. Spread the jam over the dough in the pan. Drop the reserved dough by tablespoons randomly over the jam.

**4.** Bake for 20 to 25 minutes, or until golden brown. Cool completely in the pan, then cut into bars.

# · CHEWY CHOCOLATE BARS ·

*Makes about 36 bars*

One 18.25-ounce package white
   cake mix
2 large eggs, lightly beaten
1/3 cup vegetable oil
One 14-ounce can sweetened
   condensed milk

1 cup (6 ounces) semisweet chocolate
   chips
1/4 cup (1/2 stick) unsalted butter, cut
   into pieces

**1.** Preheat the oven to 350°F. Grease a 9×13-inch baking pan.

**2.** Stir together the cake mix, eggs, and oil. With floured hands, press two-thirds of the mixture into the prepared pan. Set the remaining mixture aside.

**3.** Combine the sweetened condensed milk, chocolate chips, and butter in a microwave-safe bowl and microwave on high (100%) power for 45 seconds; stir. Microwave for 50 to 60 seconds longer, stirring at 30-second intervals, or until the chips and butter are melted; stir until smooth. Pour over the crust.

**4.** Drop teaspoonfuls of the remaining cake mixture over the top. Bake for 25 to 30 minutes, or until lightly browned. Cool completely in the pan on a wire rack before cutting into bars.

# • CHEWY DATE NUT BARS •

*Makes 36 bars*

| | |
|---|---|
| One 18.25-ounce package yellow cake mix | 2 large eggs, lightly beaten |
| $^3/_4$ cup packed light brown sugar | 2 cups chopped pitted dates |
| $^3/_4$ cup unsalted butter, melted | 2 cups chopped walnuts |

**1.** Preheat the oven to 350°F. Grease a 9×13-inch baking pan.

**2.** Combine the cake mix and brown sugar in a large bowl. Add the butter and eggs. Using an electric mixer on medium speed, beat for 2 minutes. Combine the dates and walnuts in a small bowl; stir into the batter (the batter will be stiff). Spread into the prepared pan.

**3.** Bake for 35 to 45 minutes, or until the edges are golden brown. Cool in the pan on a wire rack for 10 minutes. Run a knife around the sides of the pan to loosen; cool completely in the pan before cutting into bars.

# · CRANBERRY-SWEET POTATO BREAD ·

*Thanksgiving aromas will fill your kitchen when you whip up
this simple bread. It's excellent for autumn bake sales.*

## Makes 16 slices

**Bread**
One 15.6-ounce package cranberry
   quick-bread mix
½ teaspoon cinnamon
2 tablespoons canola oil
1 large egg
¾ cup cooked, mashed sweet
   potato

**Topping**
1 tablespoon sugar
¾ teaspoon ground cinnamon

**1.** Preheat the oven to 350°F. Grease and flour the bottom only of an 8×4-inch loaf pan.

**2.** Combine all the bread ingredients and 1 cup water in a large bowl. Stir until the mix is moistened. Pour the batter into the prepared pan.

**3.** Make the topping: Stir together the topping ingredients in a small bowl, then sprinkle over the batter.

**4.** Bake for 55 to 60 minutes, or until a toothpick inserted in the center comes out clean. Cool in the pan on a wire rack for 15 minutes, then turn out onto the rack to cool completely before cutting into slices.

# · COCONUT CHOCOLATE CHIP LOAF ·

*If you're worried that everyone will be donating chocolate chip cookies to the bake sale, try this sweet bread variation on the classic.*

*Makes 12 slices*

One 19.85-ounce package chocolate chip muffin mix
1⅓ cups toasted coconut (page 197)

1 large egg
1 teaspoon vanilla extract

**1.** Preheat the oven to 350°F. Grease and flour a 9×5×3-inch loaf pan.

**2.** Pour the muffin mix into a medium bowl and stir to break up any lumps. Add the coconut, egg, ½ cup water, and vanilla. Stir until moistened, about 50 strokes. Pour into the prepared pan.

**3.** Bake for 45 to 50 minutes, or until a toothpick inserted in the center comes out clean. Cool in the pan on a wire rack for 15 minutes before slicing.

# · BANANA GINGERBREAD MUFFINS ·

*These are delicious both warm and at room temperature.*

*Makes 16 muffins*

One 14.5-ounce package gingerbread cake and cookie mix
1 cup mashed very ripe banana (about 2 medium bananas)
³/₄ cup quick-cooking oats
2 large eggs, lightly beaten
1 teaspoon vanilla extract

**1.** Preheat the oven to 375°F. Grease the bottoms only of 16 medium muffin cups with shortening, or line with foil or paper baking cups.

**2.** Whisk together all the ingredients and ³/₄ cup water in a large bowl until well blended. Divide the batter evenly among the muffin cups.

**3.** Bake for 15 to 20 minutes, or until a toothpick inserted in the center comes out clean. Immediately remove from the pan to a wire rack to cool slightly before serving.

# · BANANA CAKE WITH PEANUT BUTTER FROSTING ·

*If you have ripe bananas on hand, this cake is a snap to make. We use a combination of mixes and pantry ingredients to give it a home-baked flavor.*

## Makes 16 slices

### Cake

One 18.25-ounce box yellow cake mix
One 3.4-ounce package vanilla
   pudding and pie filling mix
1/3 cup canola oil
1 cup mashed ripe banana (about
   2 medium bananas)
3 large eggs, lightly
   beaten

### Frosting

3/4 cup Vanilla Buttercream Frosting
   (page 171)
1/2 cup chunky peanut butter

**1.** Preheat the oven to 350° F. Grease and flour a 12-cup Bundt pan.

**2.** Combine all the cake ingredients with 1/4 cup water in a large bowl. Using an electric mixer on low speed, beat until just moistened. Increase the speed to medium and beat for 2 minutes. Pour the batter into the prepared pan.

**3.** Bake for 45 to 55 minutes, or until a toothpick inserted in the center comes out clean. (The cake will be moist on top.) Cool in the pan for 10 minutes, then turn the cake out onto a wire rack. Cool completely, at least 45 minutes. Transfer the cooled cake to a serving plate.

**4.** Place the frosting in a small microwave-safe bowl. Microwave on high (100%) power for 25 to 35 seconds, or until of thin consistency. Immediately stir in the peanut butter. Drizzle the warm frosting over the top of the cake, allowing some to drip down the sides. Let the frosting set before cutting into slices.

# Candy and Confections

*Homemade candy is not found on every bake sale table, and when it is, it's really a treat hard to pass up. The confections in this chapter are surprisingly easy to make and look attractive. Teens are especially enamored of homemade candy; it's a good bet for high school bake sales.*

# • CRANBERRY-ALMOND BARK •

*This amount of ingredients makes a sheet of chocolate measuring about 9 by 9 inches. You can break it into any size you want. We like to break the bark unevenly into 2- to 4-inch chunks.*

*Makes 20 to 24 pieces*

| | |
|---|---|
| 2 cups (12 ounces) white chocolate melts or morsels | $^2/_3$ cup whole almonds, with the skins<br>$^1/_2$ cup dried cranberries |

**1.** Line a baking sheet with wax paper or parchment paper.

**2.** Fill the bottom of a double boiler with 1 inch of water and bring to a simmer over medium heat. Melt the white chocolate in the top of the double boiler, making sure that the water doesn't touch the bottom of the bowl. Heat, stirring frequently, until the chocolate is completely melted. Remove from the heat and stir in the almonds and cranberries.

**3.** Using a rubber spatula, spread the hot white chocolate mixture on the prepared baking sheet. (It does not need to be completely even.) Refrigerate until the chocolate is firm, at least 30 minutes.

**4.** Break the bark into uneven pieces. Package several pieces together in sealable bags or colored cellophane tied with a ribbon.

# · GRAPE-NUTS BARK ·

*This one's a crunchy-chewy variation on the theme.*

*Makes 20 to 24 pieces*

2 cups (12 ounces) semisweet chocolate melts or chocolate morsels
½ cup Grape-Nuts cereal

¼ cup golden raisins
¼ cup dried cherries, blueberries, or cranberries

**1.** Line a baking sheet with wax paper or parchment paper.

**2.** Fill the bottom of a double boiler with 1 inch of water and bring to a simmer over medium heat. Melt the chocolate in the top of the double boiler, making sure that the water doesn't touch the bottom of the bowl. Heat, stirring frequently, until the chocolate is completely melted. Remove from the heat and stir in the cereal and dried fruit.

**3.** Using a rubber spatula, spread the hot chocolate mixture on the prepared baking sheet. (It does not need to be completely even.) Refrigerate until the chocolate is firm, at least 30 minutes.

**4.** Break the bark into uneven pieces. Package several pieces together in sealable bags or colored cellophane tied with a ribbon.

# · PEPPERMINT BARK ·

*A Christmas classic that's become popular all year round.*

---

*Makes 20 to 24 pieces*

| | |
|---|---|
| 2 cups (12 ounces) white chocolate melts or white chocolate morsels | ½ cup coarsely crushed peppermint candies |

**1.** Line a baking sheet with wax paper or parchment paper.

**2.** Fill the bottom of a double boiler with 1 inch of water and bring to a simmer over medium heat. Melt the white chocolate in the top of the double boiler, making sure that the water doesn't touch the bottom of the bowl. Heat, stirring frequently, until the chocolate is completely melted. Remove from the heat and stir in the crushed candy.

**3.** Using a rubber spatula, spread the hot white chocolate mixture on the prepared baking sheet. (It does not need to be completely even.) Refrigerate until the chocolate is firm, at least 30 minutes.

**4.** Break the bark into uneven pieces. Package several pieces together in resealable bags or colored cellophane tied with a red ribbon.

---

**TIP**

To crush the peppermints, unwrap the candies and place them into a sealable bag, then place that bag inside another bag. Either roll with a rolling pin or smash with a mallet or meat pounder. If there's a child handy, she or he will love the smashing job.

---

# • GINGERSNAP GOODIES •

*The classic cookies become confections in this no-bake preparation.*

## *Makes about 30 pieces*

⅓ cup confectioners' sugar
Pinch each of cinnamon and
    nutmeg
24 gingersnaps, crushed

4 tablespoons dark corn syrup, plus
    more as needed
2 tablespoons peanut butter (creamy
    or crunchy)

**1.** Line a baking sheet with wax paper or parchment paper. Stir together the confectioners' sugar and spices in a small bowl.

**2.** Combine the gingersnap crumbs, corn syrup, and peanut butter in a large bowl; stir until the mixture forms a sticky dough. (If the mixture doesn't hold together, add corn syrup a tablespoon at a time until it does.)

**3.** Scoop the mixture out by tablespoons and roll into 1-inch balls. Roll each ball in the sugar mixture and place on the prepared baking sheet.

**4.** Package them individually or in pairs in little cellophane bags tied with a ribbon.

> **TIP**
>
> The cookies for this recipe don't need to be pulverized; just put them in a sealed plastic bag and roll them with a rolling pin.

# · YUMMY PRETZEL TREATS ·

*Once the chocolate sets, these pretzels are quite sturdy. They look great served in a glass vase.*

## Makes 24 pretzels

| | |
|---|---|
| 2 cups (12 ounces) white chocolate melts | Assorted sprinkles, chopped nuts, and chopped candies, for topping |
| 2 cups (12 ounces) milk chocolate melts | 24 pretzel rods (7 to 9 inches) |

**1.** Line a baking sheet with wax paper or parchment paper.

**2.** Pour the white chocolate candy melts into a small microwave-safe bowl. Melt at medium (50%) power, stirring at 1-minute intervals. In another bowl, melt the milk chocolate melts.

**3.** Pour the toppings into the individual cups of a muffin tin.

**4.** Dip the bottom half of each pretzel into one of the chocolates, then dip into the toppings of your choice. Lay on the lined baking sheet to harden. The chocolate can be remelted in the microwave using 30-second intervals, if necessary.

> **TIP**
>
> To store, lay pretzels in a plastic container or lasagne pan with sheets of wax paper between the layers.

# · BAGS O' CHEESY POPCORN ·

*Makes about 10 bags*

| | |
|---|---|
| 8 cups unsalted popped popcorn | ½ teaspoon seasoned salt |
| 1 cup small pretzel twists | ¼ teaspoon garlic powder |
| 1 cup small cheese-flavored crackers | 1 teaspoon Worcestershire sauce |
| 3 tablespoons olive oil | ½ cup grated Parmesan cheese |

**1.** Preheat the oven to 300°F.

**2.** Combine the popcorn, pretzels, and crackers in a large bowl; toss to mix.

**3.** Stir together the oil, seasoned salt, garlic powder, Worcestershire sauce, and Parmesan. Pour over the popcorn mixture and mix well. Pour the mixture evenly into an ungreased 9×13-inch pan.

**4.** Bake for 20 to 30 minutes, stirring two or three times during baking.

**5.** Fill small sealable bags with the cheesy popcorn, using about 1 cup popcorn per bag.

# · PRIMARY-COLORED POPCORN BALLS ·

*Kids love to make popcorn balls almost as much as they love to eat them.
Just supervise them closely when working with caramel, as it bubbles
up and is very hot.*

### Makes 12 to 14 balls

8 cups unsalted popped
  popcorn
½ cup corn syrup
1 cup sugar
½ teaspoon salt
¼ cup (½ stick) unsalted butter,
  cut into chunks

1 teaspoon vanilla
  extract
Red, yellow, and blue food
  coloring

**1.** Line a baking sheet with wax paper or parchment paper. Place the popcorn in a large heatproof bowl. Set aside.

**2.** Combine the corn syrup, ⅓ cup water, the sugar, and the salt in a medium saucepan over medium heat. Stir constantly until the mixture comes to a boil, then let the mixture boil without stirring until it reaches the hard-ball stage (255°F on a candy thermometer). (If sugar crystals form on the side of the pan, carefully brush them down with a pastry brush dipped in hot water.) Remove the pan from the heat.

**3.** Carefully but vigorously stir in the butter and the vanilla. (Be aware that the mixture will bubble up strongly, but will settle down as you stir to combine.)

**4.** Use a medium heatproof bowl for each color and divide the mixture evenly among them. Immediately stir in the food coloring. Carefully stir in one-third of the popcorn. When slightly cooled, 5 to 7 minutes, shape into Ping-Pong-size balls. Place the balls on the prepared pan after shaping to let them cool completely before wrapping in plastic wrap.

TIP

To serve at your sale, wrap the balls individually in clear plastic wrap, gathered at the top and secured with red, yellow, and blue curly ribbon.

# · CARAMEL POPCORN ·

*Makes 12 clusters*

6 cups unsalted popped popcorn          1 cup firmly packed light brown
1 cup roasted peanuts                            sugar
1 tablespoon unsalted butter              $\frac{1}{4}$ cup water

**1.** Line a baking sheet with wax paper or parchment paper.

**2.** Toss the popcorn and peanuts together in a large bowl. Spread out in a single layer on the prepared baking sheet.

**3.** Melt the butter in a medium saucepan over medium heat. Add the sugar and bring to a boil, stirring frequently. Cover and cook for 3 minutes.

**4.** Uncover and cook until the soft-crack stage (275°F on a candy thermometer). Pour the hot mixture over the popcorn and peanuts. Allow to cool completely, then break into clusters.

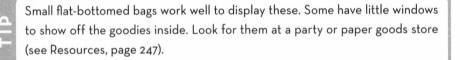

TIP: Small flat-bottomed bags work well to display these. Some have little windows to show off the goodies inside. Look for them at a party or paper goods store (see Resources, page 247).

# · WHITE CHOCOLATE-CARAMEL POPCORN BITES ·

*Makes about 6 cups*

5 cups Caramel Popcorn (page 218) or store-bought

½ cup toasted chopped pecans

3 cups (18 ounces) white chocolate melts

**1.** Line a baking sheet with wax paper or parchment paper.

**2.** Spread the popcorn on the prepared baking sheet. Sprinkle with the pecans.

**3.** Fill the bottom of a double boiler with 1 inch of water and bring to a simmer over medium heat. Melt the white chocolate in the top of the double boiler, making sure that the water doesn't touch the bottom of the bowl. Heat, stirring frequently, until the chocolate is completely melted. Drizzle the melted chocolate over the popcorn. Refrigerate for 30 minutes, then break into bite-size pieces.

TIP

These little bites are easy to transport to a bake sale in a shoebox lined with aluminum foil or wax paper.

# · WASABI SNACK MIX ·

*High school kids love the sweet and spicy zing of this addictive treat.*
*Sell it in sealable bags.*

## Makes about 10 cups

| | |
|---|---|
| ¼ cup (½ stick) unsalted butter, softened | 3 tablespoons wasabi paste |
| 1½ cups sugar | 2 tablespoons coarse salt |
| 6 cups unsalted peanuts | 3 cups wasabi peas |
| | 2 cups mini Asian rice crackers |

**1.** Preheat the oven to 350°F. Line a baking sheet with aluminum foil or parchment paper and butter the foil or parchment.

**2.** Combine the sugar and ⅔ cup water in a medium saucepan over medium heat. Bring to a boil, stirring to dissolve the sugar. Boil without stirring for 5 minutes and remove the pan from the heat.

**3.** Add the peanuts and let stand 5 minutes, stirring often.

**4.** Drain the peanuts and return them to the saucepan. Stir in the wasabi paste and salt. Then spread the peanuts in an even layer on the prepared pan.

**5.** Bake for 15 minutes, stirring twice, until golden brown. Cool completely in the pan, then toss with the wasabi peas and crackers. Fill small sealable bags with the mixture, using about 1 cup per bag.

# · SWEET GINGER PECANS ·

*Makes 3 cups*

| | |
|---|---|
| 2 tablespoons (¼ stick) unsalted butter, softened | 2 teaspoons ground ginger |
| ⅔ cup sugar | 2 teaspoons sea salt |
| 3 cups pecan halves | ¼ teaspoon cayenne pepper |

**1.** Preheat the oven to 350°F. Line a baking sheet with aluminum foil or parchment paper, and generously grease the foil or parchment with the butter.

**2.** Combine the sugar and ⅔ cup water in a medium saucepan and bring to a boil, stirring to dissolve the sugar. Boil without stirring for 5 minutes. Remove from the heat and stir in the pecans. Let stand for 5 minutes, stirring often.

**3.** Drain the pecans and return them to the saucepan. Add the ginger, salt, and cayenne and stir to coat the pecans.

**4.** Spread in a single layer on the prepared pan. Bake for 15 minutes, stirring once. Cool completely in the pan before putting into cups or bags.

TIP

These are easy to serve by the cup. They look great in small paper party cups available at party stores (see Resources, page 247). Or use cupcake liners.

# · TOFFEE MARSHMALLOW DELIGHTS ·

*Makes 30 pieces*

4 cups Special-K cereal
Three 2-ounce toffee bars, broken
   up into pieces
²/₃ cup sweetened condensed milk
¼ cup (½ stick) unsalted butter
30 large marshmallows

**1.** Line a baking sheet with wax paper. Pour the cereal in a medium bowl.

**2.** Combine the toffee, sweetened condensed milk, and butter in a small heavy saucepan over medium heat. Stir until the toffee is melted and the mixture is smooth. Remove from the heat.

**3.** Using a fork, dip one marshmallow in the toffee mixture until coated, letting the excess toffee drip back into the pan. (If the toffee mixture becomes too thick for dipping, reheat over medium heat until it returns to the desired consistency.)

**4.** Roll a toffee-coated marshmallow in the cereal until coated; then, using a second fork, push the marshmallow off onto the prepared pan. Repeat with the remaining marshmallows, toffee mixture, and cereal. Let the marshmallows stand until set, about 20 minutes.

**TIP** Arrange the marshmallows on a colorful plate. Place a party toothpick in each one, and people can help themselves. Two for a dollar usually works.

# · ALI'S TREATS ·

*These fun bars come all the way from friends in Brockville, Ontario. Thanks, Hess family!*

*Makes 3 to 4 dozen bars*

1 bag (12 ounces) mini marshmallows

2 cups (12 ounces) semisweet chocolate chips

1 cup creamy peanut butter

$^3/_4$ cup unsalted butter

2 teaspoons vanilla extract

**1.** Spray a 9×13-inch baking pan with baking spray. Layer the pan with the marshmallows.

**2.** Melt the chocolate chips, peanut butter, and butter in the microwave on medium (50%) power for 2 to 3 minutes. Stir to combine. Allow to cool for at least 10 minutes. Stir in the vanilla.

**3.** Pour the chocolate mixture over the marshmallows and stir to distribute. Spread evenly in the pan. Cool in the fridge or freezer for at least 1 hour and up to overnight before cutting into bars.

**TIP**

If you have a freezer nearby, sell these frozen—they are even better that way, and fly off the table.

# Ten

## Holiday Tables

Bake sales often coincide with holidays, so we've included a handful of our favorite treats for those special occasions. The baking aisle of the supermarket makes it easy to customize baked goods for a holiday, with colored morsels, sprinkles, cupcake liners, sugars, icings, and more.

# • VALENTINE'S DAY LOVE COOKIES •

*Colored candy melts are a great invention: They are supereasy to use, and make baked goods and candies look amazing. They're available at baking-supply stores and websites (see Resources, page 247). Here we use them to make lovely red Valentine's Day cookies.*

*Makes about 3½ dozen hearts*

| | |
|---|---|
| ¾ cup sugar | 1 large egg, lightly beaten |
| 1 cup plus 2 tablespoons (2¼ sticks) unsalted butter, softened | 2 teaspoons vanilla extract |
| One 3-ounce package cream cheese, softened | 3 cups unbleached all-purpose flour, plus more for rolling out dough |
| | 1 cup red candy melts |

**1.** Combine the sugar, 1 cup butter, the cream cheese, egg, and vanilla in a large bowl. Using an electric mixer on medium speed, beat until light and fluffy, stopping to scrape the bowl often.

**2.** Add the flour; beat on low speed until well mixed. Divide the dough in half and wrap each half in wax paper. Refrigerate for 2 hours or until firm.

**3.** Preheat the oven to 375°F. Roll out half of the dough to 1¼ inch thick on a lightly floured surface. Cut out cookies with lightly floured heart-shaped cookie cutters and place 1 inch apart on ungreased baking sheets. Repeat with the other half of the dough. Bake for 7 to 10 minutes, or until the edges are very lightly browned. Transfer immediately to wire racks to cool completely.

**4.** Line the cooled baking sheets with wax paper. Heat the candy melts and the remaining 2 tablespoons butter in a small saucepan over low heat for 4 to 5 minutes, or until melted. Dip half of each heart into the melted candy mixture. Place on the prepared baking sheets and refrigerate for 1 hour or until the coating is firm.

**5.** Store, covered, in the refrigerator for up to 5 days.

# · SWEET NOTHING BARS ·

*Conversation hearts are those candies with cute sayings on them that have become ubiquitous around Valentine's Day.*

## Makes 25 bars

| | |
|---|---|
| 5 tablespoons unsalted butter | 6 cups frosted oat cereal with marshmallow bits |
| 40 large marshmallows | 1 cup conversation hearts |

**1.** Line a 9×13-inch baking pan with aluminum foil and spray the foil with cooking spray.

**2.** Melt the butter and marshmallows in a medium saucepan over medium heat, stirring constantly until melted and smooth, about 3 minutes. Remove from the heat.

**3.** Stir in the cereal and candy. Pour into the prepared pan and press evenly onto the bottom using a greased rubber spatula or your hands (coat them with butter first). Let stand for 30 minutes, or until completely cool, before cutting into bars.

# • ST. PATRICK'S MINI SODA BREADS •

*Makes 12 to 14 soda breads*

| | |
|---|---|
| 1½ cups unbleached all-purpose flour, plus more for kneading dough | ¼ cup (½ stick) unsalted butter, softened |
| ¾ teaspoon baking soda | 1½ teaspoons caraway seeds |
| ¾ teaspoon baking powder | 1 large egg yolk |
| ½ teaspoon salt | ½ cup buttermilk |
| | ¼ cup honey |

**1.** Preheat the oven to 350°F. Line a baking sheet with parchment paper or spray with baking spray.

**2.** Combine the flour, baking soda, baking powder, and salt in a large bowl. Add the butter and, using an electric mixer on low speed, beat until the mixture resembles coarse meal. Stir in the caraway seeds.

**3.** Whisk together the egg yolk, buttermilk, and honey in a small bowl. Add the egg mixture to the flour mixture and stir just until the dry ingredients are moistened. Do not overmix.

**4.** Turn out the dough onto a lightly floured work surface and gently knead once or twice until the dough comes together. Gently roll the dough to ½ inch thick. Dip a 1½-inch biscuit cutter into flour and cut as many rounds as you can. Transfer the rounds to the prepared pan. Gather the scraps, reroll, and cut more rounds with the remaining dough.

**5.** Bake until the rounds have risen and are light golden, 10 to 12 minutes. Transfer to a wire rack and let cool for 5 minutes.

> **TIP** Avoid twisting the cutter as you press it into the dough. Press it straight down and pull it straight up. This makes the biscuits rise higher.

# · TRADITIONAL PASSOVER MACAROONS ·

*Delicious as is, or you can dip these cookies in chocolate glaze*
*for a fancier treat.*

---

## *Makes about 24 cookies*

$^3/_4$ cup sugar

2$^1/_2$ cups unsweetened flaked coconut

2 large egg whites

1 teaspoon vanilla extract

$^1/_8$ teaspoon salt

**1.** Preheat the oven to 375°F. Spray a baking sheet with cooking spray (not baking spray) and set aside.

**2.** Combine the sugar, coconut, egg whites, vanilla, and salt in a medium bowl and mix with a rubber spatula.

**3.** Scoop out the mixture by heaping tablespoons onto the prepared baking sheet, spacing about 2 inches apart.

**4.** Bake until golden, 10 to 12 minutes. Transfer immediately to a wire rack and cool completely.

**TIP** Macaroons will keep at room temperature in an airtight container for up to 1 week.

# • EASTER BASKET CUPCAKES •

*These are perfect for a church bake sale or a spring fair. Pastel-colored frostings, candies, and cupcake liners are usually plentiful in markets in the month or two leading up to the holiday.*

---

### Makes 24 cupcakes

24 vanilla cupcakes (page 166), baked and cooled
1 recipe Seven-Minute Frosting (page 173), or one 1-pound can white chocolate frosting, tinted in pastel colors

24 Twizzlers, pastel-colored if available (or red, if not), cut so they fit the cupcake when bent into a U shape
120 mini jellybeans, assorted colors

**1.** Frost the cupcakes, making a thick layer on the top.

**2.** Using a small spoon, make a depression in the center of the frosting on each cupcake. Fill each depression with 5 jellybeans.

**3.** Bend a Twizzler into a U shape and press the ends into each side of a cupcake, to look like handles. Be sure the ends are inserted into the cake (and not just the frosting), so they will stay in. Repeat with the remaining licorice and cupcakes.

# · HALLOWEEN PARTY PRETZELS ·

*Makes 24 pretzels*

2 cups (12 ounces) white chocolate
melts
2 cups (12 ounces) milk chocolate
melts
Black and orange sprinkles

Halloween candies, such as candy
corn, black and orange gumdrops,
and black and orange jelly beans,
chopped
Chopped nuts
24 pretzel rods (7 to 9 inches)

**1.** Line a baking sheet with wax paper.

**2.** Microwave the white chocolate candy melts in a microwave-safe bowl on medium (50%) power, stirring at 30-second intervals, until melted, about 2 minutes. In another bowl, melt the milk chocolate candy melts.

**3.** Pour each topping into a plate or wide shallow bowl. While the melts are still warm, dip the end of the pretzel in and immediately roll in the candy or nut toppings of your choice. Place on the wax paper and let stand until the chocolate has hardened, about 20 minutes.

# • MUMMY CUPCAKES •

*Another Halloween treat, these cupcakes scream "Mummy!" Rolled fondant is easy to use and available at most craft stores or baking-supply stores.*

## Makes 24 cupcakes

1 recipe Vanilla Buttercream
  Frosting (page 171)
24 vanilla cupcakes (page 166), baked
  in white liners and cooled

One 1-pound package white fondant,
  prerolled
48 chocolate chips

**1.** Frost the cupcakes with the white frosting, reserving about ¼ cup.

**2.** Lay the prerolled white fondant on your work surface and roll out as thin as possible.

**3.** Using a knife or pizza cutter, cut the fondant into ¼-inch-wide strips, then cut these strips into 1- to 3-inch pieces. Lay the fondant strips across the cupcake, overlapping some at slightly different angles so they look like a mummy's bandages. Make two dots with white frosting and press chocolate chips into them, point side down, for eyes.

# · PEANUT BUTTER GHOST COOKIES ·

*Makes 3 dozen cookies*

One 16-ounce package vanilla
candy melts
One 1-pound package peanut-shaped
sandwich cookies

72 mini chocolate
morsels

**1.** Line two baking sheets with wax paper. Following the package directions, melt the vanilla candy melts in a microwave-safe bowl. Stir until smooth.

**2.** Using small kitchen tongs, dip each cookie into the melted candy, turning to coat evenly. Let any excess coating drip into the bowl, then place on the prepared baking sheets. While the coating is still wet, place two morsels on the cookie for eyes. Let stand for 15 minutes, or until the coating is set.

# · CHRISTMAS GRAHAM BARS ·

*Makes 32 bars*

| | |
|---|---|
| 8 cups honey graham cereal squares | 1/3 cup unsalted butter |
| 2 cups small red and green gum drops | 1/4 cup honey |
| 2 cups (12 ounces) white vanilla morsels | One 10-ounce package marshmallows |

**1.** Spray a 9×13-inch baking pan with cooking spray. Combine the cereal squares and gum drops in a large bowl.

**2.** Combine the vanilla morsels, butter, and honey in a large saucepan. Cook, stirring, over low heat until melted and smooth. Add the marshmallows and stir until melted.

**3.** Pour the marshmallow mixture over the cereal mixture in the bowl; fold gently to mix. Turn into the prepared pan. Spray a rubber spatula with cooking spray and use it to spread the mixture evenly in the pan. Let stand for 20 minutes and cut into bars.

# • CANDY CANE COOKIES •

*Makes about 4½ dozen cookies*

| | |
|---|---|
| 2½ cups unbleached all-purpose flour | 1 cup confectioners' sugar |
| 1 teaspoon baking powder | 1 large egg |
| ½ teaspoon salt | 1 teaspoon almond extract |
| 1 cup (2 sticks) unsalted butter, softened | 1 teaspoon vanilla extract |
| | ¼ teaspoon peppermint extract |
| | ½ teaspoon liquid red food coloring |

**1.** Preheat the oven to 350°F. Lightly grease baking sheets with baking spray or butter. Combine the flour, baking powder, and salt in a medium bowl.

**2.** Using an electric mixer on medium speed, beat the butter, sugar, egg, and extracts in a large bowl until light and creamy.

**3.** Add the flour mixture to the butter mixture and stir until a stiff dough forms. Divide the dough into two equal portions.

**4.** Knead the food coloring into one portion of dough until evenly tinted. Scoop out about 1 teaspoon of each color dough and roll each color into a 5½-inch rope. Lay the ropes side by side, pinch both ends together, and twist. Form the twist into a candy cane shape. Repeat with the remaining dough. Place the canes about 2 inches apart on the prepared baking sheets.

**5.** Bake for about 10 minutes, or until just golden. Cool on the baking sheets for 5 minutes, then transfer to wire racks to cool completely.

**TIP** If you have room on your bake sale table, hang these from a small tree to display them.

# · PEPPERMINT PINWHEELS ·

*Makes about 8 dozen cookies*

1 cup confectioners' sugar
1 cup (2 sticks) unsalted butter, softened
1½ teaspoons almond extract
1 teaspoon vanilla extract
1 large egg
2½ cups unbleached all-purpose flour, plus more for rolling out dough

½ teaspoon salt
¼ teaspoon liquid red food coloring
Granulated sugar, for sprinkling

*Glaze*
1 cup confectioners' sugar
1 tablespoon light corn syrup
¼ cup finely crushed hard peppermint candy, for garnish

**1.** Mix the confectioners' sugar, butter, almond extract, vanilla, and egg in a medium bowl. Stir in the flour and salt. Divide the dough in half. Stir the food coloring into one half of the dough until evenly colored. Cover and refrigerate 1 hour, or until firm.

**2.** Roll out each half of the dough on a lightly floured surface to an 8-inch square. Place the red square on the plain square and roll out to a 12-inch square. Roll into a tight log. Wrap with plastic wrap and refrigerate for 2 hours, or until firm.

**3.** Preheat the oven to 375°F. Cut the roll into ⅛-inch-thick slices. Place the slices about 1 inch apart on ungreased baking sheets. Sprinkle lightly with granulated sugar. Bake for 7 to 9 minutes, or until the edges are light brown.

**4.** While the cookies are baking, make the glaze: Combine the confectioners' sugar and corn syrup in a small bowl. Stir in 3½ teaspoons warm water until smooth. Spread a thin layer of glaze on each cookie and sprinkle crushed peppermint candy on the wet glaze. Let stand until set, about 20 minutes.

# · RED, WHITE, AND GREEN COOKIES ·

*Makes 2½ dozen cookies*

| | |
|---|---|
| One 18-ounce package refrigerated cookie dough | Red food coloring |
| ¼ teaspoon peppermint extract, divided | Green food coloring |

**1.** Remove the dough from the wrapper. Cut the dough into three equal sections.

**2.** Combine one-third of the dough, ⅛ teaspoon peppermint extract, and red food coloring. Knead the dough until evenly tinted the desired shade of red, adding more food coloring if necessary.

**3.** Repeat with the second one-third of the dough, remaining ⅛ teaspoon peppermint extract, and the green food coloring. Leave the remaining third of the dough plain.

**4.** Roll each portion of dough into an 8-inch log. Place the red log beside the green log; press together. Place the plain log on top, like a pyramid. Press the logs together to form one tricolored roll; wrap in plastic wrap and roll along a flat surface to smooth the sides. Chill for 2 hours or overnight.

**5.** Preheat the oven to 350°F. Slice the dough into ¼-inch-thick slices and place the slices 2 inches apart on ungreased baking sheets. Bake for 8 to 9 minutes, or until set but not browned. Cool for 1 minute on the baking sheets, then transfer to wire racks to cool completely.

# · CHOCOLATE CHUNK CHRISTMAS CAKE ·

*These loaves make great gifts and sell well at Christmas fairs. To add to the appeal of the gift, attach small decorative tags listing the ingredients to the loaves. They keep well for up to a month in the refrigerator.*

## *Makes three 8×4-inch loaves*

| | |
|---|---|
| 1 cup raisins | 1 teaspoon ground ginger |
| 3 cups golden raisins | $3/4$ teaspoon salt |
| $1/3$ cup chopped candied pineapple | $1/2$ teaspoon ground nutmeg |
| 1 cup chopped pitted dates | $1/2$ teaspoon ground cloves |
| 1 cup slivered blanched almonds | $1 1/4$ cups firmly packed light brown |
| 2 cups (12 ounces) semisweet | sugar |
| chocolate morsels | 1 cup (2 sticks) unsalted butter, |
| 1 cup (6 ounces) white | softened |
| chocolate morsels | 6 large eggs |
| 3 cups unbleached all-purpose flour | $1/4$ cup molasses |
| $1 1/2$ teaspoons baking powder | $1/2$ cup cold strong coffee |
| 2 teaspoons ground cinnamon | |

**1.** Preheat the oven to 300°F. Generously grease and flour three 8×4-inch loaf pans. Combine the raisins, golden raisins, pineapple, dates, almonds, and chocolate in a very large bowl.

**2.** Spoon the flour into a measuring cup and level off with the back of a knife. Combine the flour, baking powder, cinnamon, ginger, salt, nutmeg, and cloves in a medium bowl; mix well. Sprinkle the mixture over the fruit and toss to coat and separate the fruit. Set aside.

**3.** Using an electric mixer on medium speed, beat the brown sugar and butter until light and fluffy. Add the eggs, one at a time, beating well after each addition. Stir in the molasses. Pour the batter over the fruit mixture and mix well. Stir in the coffee until well mixed. Divide evenly among the prepared pans.

**4.** Bake for $1\frac{1}{4}$ to $1\frac{1}{2}$ hours, or until deep golden brown and a toothpick inserted in the center comes out clean. Cool in the pans for 15 minutes, then transfer to a wire rack to cool completely. Wrap tightly in plastic wrap or aluminum foil.

**NOTE:** Loaves will keep for 1 month in the refrigerator and up to 3 months in the freezer.

❝ I made these for a sale at the Holiday Crafts Fair at my son's school two weeks before Christmas. Each sold for $12, and half the proceeds went to the PTA. People seemed to feel good supporting the school as they shopped. ❞

—Tanya S., Dallas, Texas

# · EDIBLE DREIDELS ·

*These are so cute and so easy to make. You can write the Hebrew letters on the sides of the marshmallows with decorating gel or frosting.*

## Makes 20 dreidels

¼ cup vanilla frosting, plus more for letters (if desired)
20 chocolate Kisses, unwrapped
20 marshmallows

10 pretzel sticks, broken in half
Blue and yellow dragées or blue and yellow sprinkles
Decorating gel (optional)

**1.** Line a baking sheet with wax paper. Stir 1 to 3 teaspoons water into the frosting to thin slightly. Using the frosting as glue, stick a Kiss to one flat side of every marshmallow. Place on the prepared baking sheet and let stand for 30 minutes, or until set.

**2.** Push a broken pretzel stick, broken side first, into the other flat side of each marshmallow.

**3.** Spread a little thinned frosting on two sides of the marshmallows and press the decorations to the sides. Let stand until set, at least 30 minutes. Draw Hebrew letters with decorating gel or frosting, if desired.

# · HOLIDAY POPCORN BALLS ·

*We like to wrap these popcorn balls in clear plastic wrap and pile them up in a big bowl. The different colors look great together. At a recent bake sale we had two full bowls of balls at each end of the table.*

## Makes 12 to 14 balls

½ cup light corn syrup

1 cup sugar

½ teaspoon salt

¼ cup (½ stick) unsalted butter, cut into cubes, plus more for your hands

1 teaspoon vanilla extract

Food coloring in holiday colors of your choice

8 cups unsalted popped popcorn

**1.** Line a baking sheet with wax paper.

**2.** Combine the corn syrup, ⅓ cup water, sugar, and salt in a medium saucepan over medium heat. Stir constantly until the mixture comes to a boil. If sugar crystals form on the side of the pan, brush them with a pastry brush dipped in hot water. Cook until a candy thermometer registers the hard-ball stage (255°F). Remove from the heat.

**3.** Stir in the butter and the vanilla. Quickly divide the mixture among bowls (one for each color) and stir in drops of food coloring to reach the desired color. Stir in the popcorn and let cool slightly, about 10 minutes. Shape into 3-inch balls, place on the prepared pan, and let stand for about 20 minutes, or until completely cool.

# · DECK THE HALLS CUPCAKES ·

*We like to use fresh mint leaves here, but you can get the same effect with premade marzipan leaves or tinted fondant.*

## Makes 24 cupcakes

1 recipe Vanilla Buttercream
    Frosting (page 171)
24 vanilla or chocolate cupcakes
    (pages 166 and 167), baked and
    cooled

2 cups sweetened flaked
    coconut
72 mint leaves
Approximately 100 Red Hots

**1.** Frost the cupcakes with the vanilla frosting. Sprinkle with the coconut.

**2.** Using a rolling pin, flatten the mint leaves. Use a mini cookie cutter in the shape of a holly leaf to cut the leaves into holly shapes.

**3.** Place three leaves on each cupcake. Dot with the Red Hots to look like holly berries.

**NOTE:** Don't place the leaves on the iced cupcakes until just before the sale.

# Special Diets

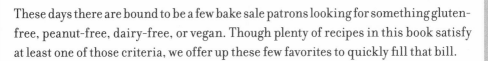

These days there are bound to be a few bake sale patrons looking for something gluten-free, peanut-free, dairy-free, or vegan. Though plenty of recipes in this book satisfy at least one of those criteria, we offer up these few favorites to quickly fill that bill.

### GLUTEN-FREE PEANUT BUTTER COOKIES · Makes about 2 dozen cookies

These flourless cookies are very easy to prepare and taste surprisingly good given the simplicity of the ingredients.

*1 large egg*
*1 cup sugar*
*1 teaspoon vanilla extract*
*1 cup creamy peanut butter*

1. Line baking sheets with parchment paper.

2. Using an electric mixer on medium speed, beat the egg, sugar, and vanilla in a large bowl until smooth. Stir in the peanut butter until smooth. Cover and refrigerate for 20 minutes.

3. Preheat the oven to 350°F. Scoop a heaping tablespoonful of dough and roll it between your palms to form a ball. Place the balls on the prepared pans, leaving about 3 inches between each cookie. Press each cookie with the back of a fork twice in opposite directions to make a crisscross pattern.

4. Bake for 12 to 15 minutes, or until lightly browned. Cool on the pan for 5 minutes, then carefully slide the entire parchment sheet (with the cookies) from the pan to a wire rack to cool completely.

**NOTE:** Cookies will keep at room temperature in an airtight container for 4 to 5 days.

## PEANUT-FREE CHOCOLATE MACAROONS · Makes about 30 cookies

These delicious cookies are great the day they are made, but we also like how chewy they get after a day or two.

*3 cups sweetened flaked coconut*
*½ cup sugar*
*6 tablespoons unbleached all-purpose flour*
*4 large egg whites*
*1½ teaspoons vanilla extract*
*½ cup finely chopped almonds*
*2 squares (2 ounces) milk chocolate*

1. Preheat the oven to 350°F. Line baking sheets with parchment paper.

2. Combine the coconut, sugar, and flour in a large bowl. Add the egg whites and vanilla and mix well. Stir in the almonds.

3. Scoop the mixture out by heaping tablespoons and place 2 inches apart on the prepared baking sheets. Flatten slightly.

4. Bake for 8 to 12 minutes, or until golden around edges. Cool the cookies completely on the sheets, then transfer to a wire rack.

5. Line the baking sheets with fresh wax paper. Heat the chocolate in the microwave at medium (50%) power, stirring at 30-second intervals, until melted, up to 2 minutes. Let cool slightly, then drizzle over the cooled cookies. Transfer to the lined baking sheets and refrigerate until the chocolate is set, about 5 minutes.

## VEGAN CARROT CUPCAKES · Makes 24 cupcakes

*1¼ cups unbleached all-purpose flour*
*1½ teaspoons baking soda*
*1½ teaspoons baking powder*
*½ teaspoon ground cinnamon*
*¼ teaspoon ground nutmeg*

¹⁄₂ teaspoon salt
1¹⁄₄ cups granulated sugar
²⁄₃ cup vegetable oil
²⁄₃ cup vanilla soy yogurt
2 cups grated carrots
¹⁄₂ cup raisins

**Cream Cheese Frosting**
¹⁄₂ cup (1 stick) margarine
¹⁄₂ cup vegan cream cheese
4 cups confectioners' sugar, sifted
2 teaspoons vanilla extract

1. Preheat the oven to 350°F. Line two 12-cup cupcake pans with paper liners. Stir together the flour, baking soda, baking powder, cinnamon, nutmeg, and salt in a medium bowl. Set aside.

2. Using an electric mixer at medium speed, beat the sugar, oil, and yogurt until well blended, about 2 minutes. Add the mixture to the dry ingredients and stir until just combined. Fold in the carrots and raisins.

3. Divide the batter among the paper liners, filling each one two-thirds full. Bake until the cupcakes spring back to the touch when pressed gently in the center, 25 to 30 minutes. Cool in the pans for 10 minutes.

4. Make the frosting: Using an electric mixer on high speed, cream the margarine and cream cheese together until fluffy, about 2 minutes. Add the confectioners' sugar and beat on low speed until combined. Stir in the vanilla. Frost the cupcakes.

**TIP:** For dairy-free treats, try any of the Rice Krispie Treats recipes in Chapter 1, substituting margarine for butter.

# · RESOURCES ·

You'll find most of what you need to pull off a bake sale at party-store and cake-supply shops. We also like to collect little (nonedible) decorations from toy shops that are often perfect for the top of a cupcake or cake. Try your local bakery for homemade edible decorations. Often they will sell you the candies they use for decorating, as well as cookie or pie dough. Below are some of our favorite online places.

**Orientaltrading.com** Party supplies in bulk, including paper goods, tablecloths, and cake or cupcake toppers.

**Partypro.com** Tableware in a multitude of themes and colors.

**Candyfavorites.com** An online candy warehouse with 2,800 items, including retro candy and lots of holiday-decorating treats.

**PastryChefCentral.com** Good assortment of baking supplies, including candy molds and chocolates for baking.

**Wilton.com** Fondant, cupcake papers, cupcake carriers, decorating sets. Wilton is a one-stop baking-supply shop. Their products are also sold at craft stores such as Michael's.

**Kitchenkrafts.com** Cake and pie boxes, cupcake stands, and cleverly themed cookie cutters make this site indispensable for bake sale regulars.

For more information on the Great American Bake Sale, organized by the nonprofit group Share Our Strength, visit www.greatamericanbakesale.org.

# INDEX